Knowles Shaw

Morning Star

A collection of new sacred songs, for the Sunday School, prayer meeting,

and the social circle

Knowles Shaw

Morning Star

A collection of new sacred songs, for the Sunday School, prayer meeting, and the social circle

ISBN/EAN: 9783337265458

Printed in Europe, USA, Canada, Australia, Japan

Cover: Foto ©Lupo / pixelio.de

More available books at **www.hansebooks.com**

THE MORNING STAR

A COLLECTION OF NEW SACRED SONGS

FOR THE

Sunday School,

PRAYER MEETING, AND THE SOCIAL CIRCLE.

BY

KNOWLES SHAW,

Author of "Shining Pearls," "Sparkling Jewels," "Golden Gate," and "

CENTRAL BOOK CONCERN,
CINCINNATI, O.   OSKALOOSA

PREFACE.

NEARLY three years have elapsed since the author's last Sunday-school work was published. His extended acquaintance, as an Evangelist, warrants the statement, that he knows the demand of the age in Sunday-school music; and his experience as an author, for ten years, during which time he has written five books, having a circulation of many thousands, enables him to supply this demand. "THE MORNING STAR" is, therefore, a collection of Sacred Songs, mostly new and original, intended to meet the wants of the Sunday-school, Social Meeting, and Family Circle, containing, as it does, five departments:—Songs of Jesus, Invitation Songs, Songs of Comfort and Joy, Practical Songs, Temperance and Miscellaneous Songs, interspersed with some of the grand old standard pieces that never wear out. We have sedulously avoided all unscriptural sentiments, admitting no piece which breathes not pure gospel truth.

All contributors to the Morning Star have been duly credited where their compositions appear, but we here render our thanks for the same.

This book is the author's own copyright property, and all who may desire to use any of the pieces must obtain written permission from him.

The Morning Star is now sent on its mission of light and comfort, praying the blessing of God upon it, and hoping that many may be led by the rays of "*The Bright Morning Star,*" which first shone in "*The Manger of Bethlehem,*" to "*Believe*" in Him who was "*On the Cross,*" but now reigns "*King of kings*"— who is "*Coming again*" to receive all who obey Him to Himself, to reign in the "Kingdom of Glory" forever.

KNOWLES SHAW.

COPYRIGHT, 1877, BY KNOWLES SHAW.

Electrotyped at Franklin Type Foundry, Cin., O.

THE MORNING STAR.

No. 1.   THE BRIGHT MORNING STAR.

"I am the root and the offspring of David, and the bright and morning star."—Rev. 22: 16.

K. SHAW.   KNOWLES SHAW.

1. Oh, sing of the "Bright Morning Star," That arose on the world's deepest gloom;
2. Its rays are resplendently grand, And it shineth in ev - ery clime;
3. That star now is shining for thee, O sin-ner, be led by its light;
4. The morning of joy draweth near, The night will soon vanish away;
5. Oh, sing of that heavenly home, "Where life everlasting shall be;"

By faith we can see it a-far, Be-yond the dark shades of the tomb.
A light from Immanuel's land, Undimmed by the cycles of time.
Where Je-sus forever shall be, In glo-ry where cometh no night.
When the Bright Morning Star will appear, To bring in that glorious day.
O Lord, our de-liverer, come, And bid us a welcome to Thee.

CHORUS.

Oh, sing of that beau-ti-ful gem, Lovely star of Bethle-hem;
Shine on my soul from worlds afar, Beautiful, "Bright and Morning Star."

No. 2. WHAT COULD WE DO WITHOUT JESUS?

"Lord, to whom shall we go? Thou hast the words of eternal life."—John 6: 68.

E. R. LATTA.   KNOWLES SHAW.

1. What could we do with-out Je-sus? What could the children do?
2. What could we do with-out Je-sus? What could the sin-ner do?
3. What could we do with-out Je-sus? What could the Christian do?

With the long pathway be-fore them, Hid-den from mortal view;
Where could he go for sal-va-tion? Who could his heart re-new?
Is there a friend or a bro-ther E-qual-ly kind and true?

How could their footsteps be guided? Sure-ly their feet would stray;
No oth-er name has been giv-en; On-ly his blood can a-tone;
In the dark hour of tempt-a-tion; In the dread hour of pain;

But that the mer-ci-ful Sav-ior Ten-der-ly leads the way.
Sin-ners can trust but in Je-sus, Claiming no worth their own.
What but the mer-cy of Je-sus Can our sad hearts sus-tain?

CHORUS.

What could we do without Je-sus? What could we do? where could we fly?

WHAT COULD WE DO? Concluded.

What could we do with-out Je-sus, When we are called to die?

No. 3.   BLOOD-BOUGHT.

"The precious blood of Christ as a lamb without spot."—1 Pet. 1: 19.

D. C. A.   D. C. ADDISON.

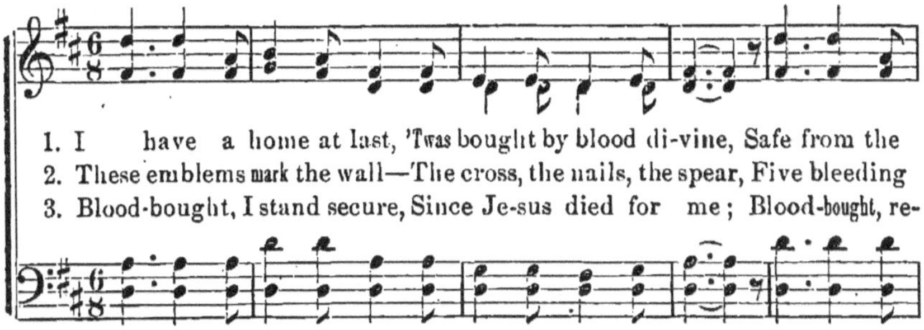

1. I have a home at last, 'Twas bought by blood di-vine, Safe from the
2. These emblems mark the wall—The cross, the nails, the spear, Five bleeding
3. Blood-bought, I stand secure, Since Je-sus died for me; Blood-bought, re-

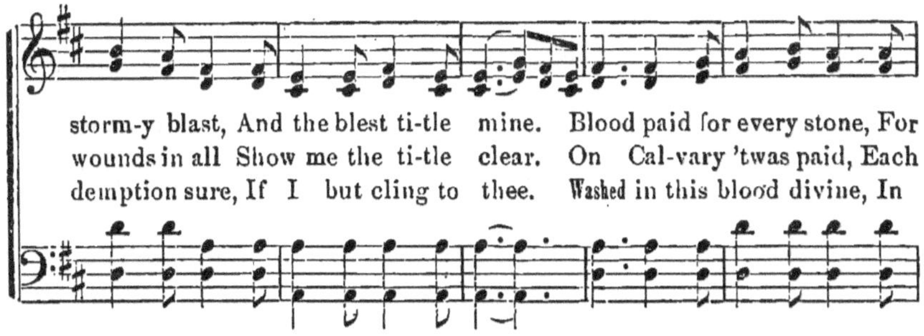

storm-y blast, And the blest ti-tle mine. Blood paid for every stone, For
wounds in all Show me the ti-tle clear. On Cal-vary 'twas paid, Each
demption sure, If I but cling to thee. Washed in this blood divine, In

roof, and nail, and door; There death is nev-er known, But life for ev-er-more.
drop to Justice due; And Love divine there laid The price for me and you.
glo - ry to ap-pear; Like him forever shine, His welcome voice to hear.

No. 5. THE MANGER OF BETHLEHEM.

"*Ye shall find the babe wrapped in swaddling clothes lying in a manger.*"—Luke 2: 12.

Dr. J. G. Holland.   Knowles Shaw.

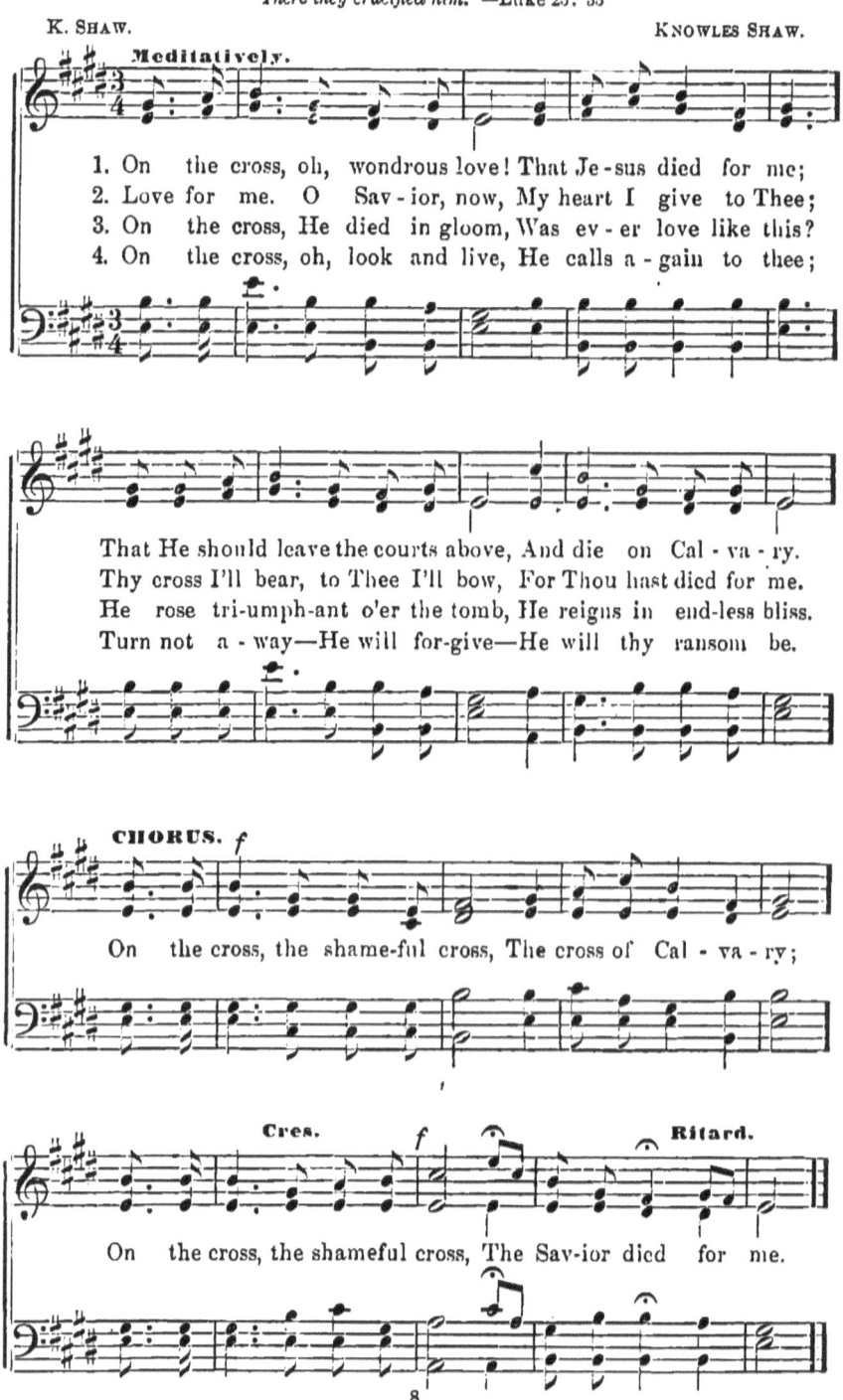

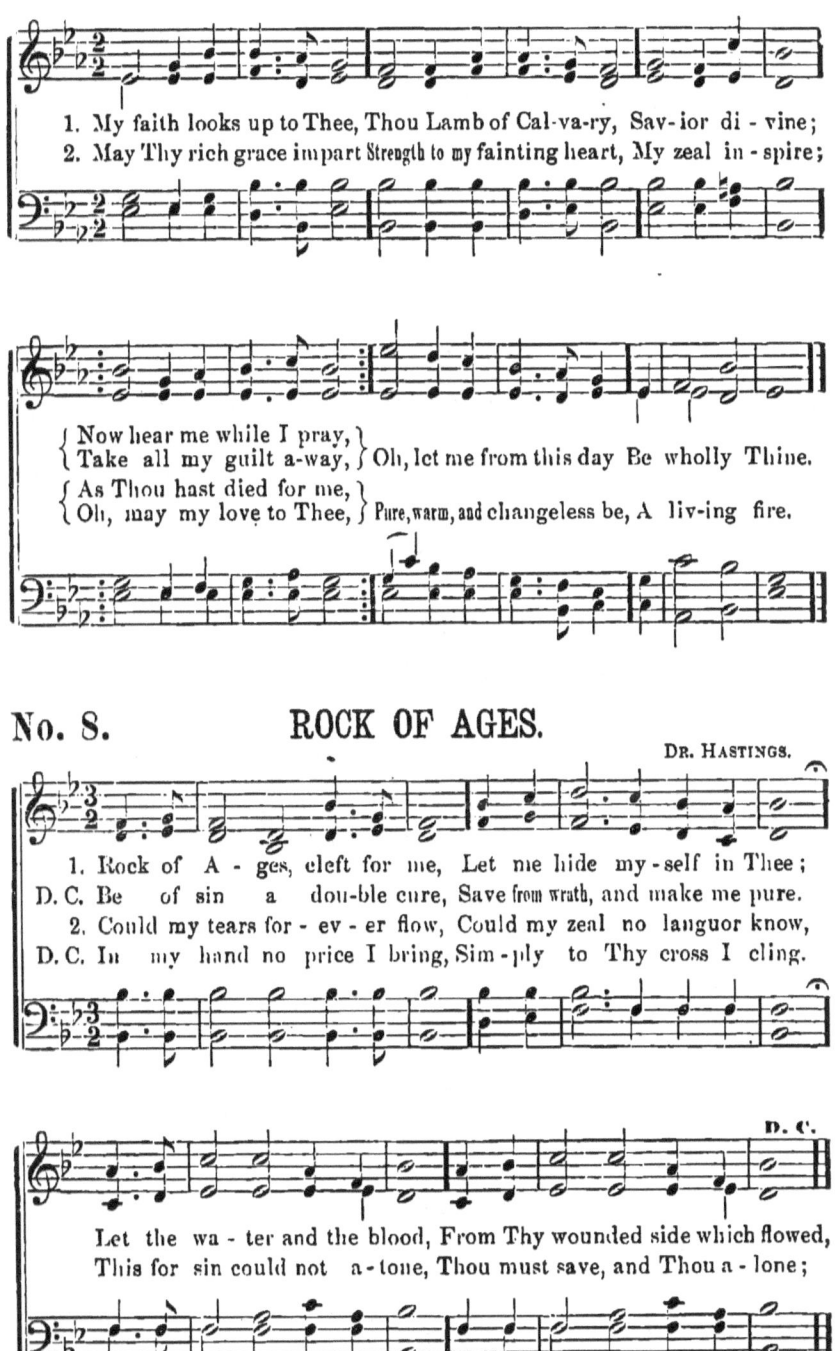

No. 9. AT THE TOMB.

"But Mary stood without at the sepulcher weeping."—John 20: 11.

K. SHAW.   KNOWLES SHAW.

1. To the tomb where they laid Him, At the dawn of the day, Mary came with her spi-ces, There her homage to pay. She had thought there to find Him, In the cold, silent tomb, And her heart filled with anguish, When she knew He had gone.

2. By His grave she stood weeping, Filled with sorrow and gloom, But she gazed on the an-gels, In the midst of the tomb. As she turned, a voice addressed her, "Why this weeping, tell me, pray?" Oh, where have you laid Him? I will take Him away.

After 2d verse.
SOLO, or DUET. *pp*   **Joyfully.**

"Ma-ry! Ma-ry!" "*Rabboni*," oh, my Master! He is ris'n from the dead.

FULL CHORUS, with great joy.

Hal-le-lu-jah! hal-le-lujah! We will praise Him, we will praise Him;

AT THE TOMB. Concluded.

No. 10.   CORONATION.

HOLDEN.

1. All hail the pow'r of Je-sus' name, Let an-gels prostrate fall;
2. Let ev-ery kindred, ev-ery tribe, On this ter-res-trial ball,
3. Oh, that with yon-der sa-cred throng, We at His feet may fall!

Bring forth the roy-al di-a-dem, And crown Him Lord of all;
To Him all maj-es-ty ascribe, And crown Him Lord of all;
We'll join the ev-er-lasting song, And crown Him Lord of all;

Bring forth the roy-al di-a-dem, And crown Him Lord of all.
To Him all maj-es-ty ascribe, And crown Him Lord of all.
We'll join the ev-er-last-ing song, And crown Him Lord of all.

No. 12.   WE BELIEVE.

"We also believe, and therefore speak."—2 Cor. 4: 13.

A Favorite in England.   KNOWLES SHAW.

1. We saw Thee not when Thou didst come To this poor world of sin and death;
2. We saw Thee not when lifted high, A-mid that wild and savage crew;
3. We gazed not in the open tomb, Where once Thy mangled body lay;
4. We walked not with the chosen few, Who saw Thee from the earth ascend;

Nor yet beheld Thy cottage home, In that de-spis-ed Naz-a-reth;
Nor heard we that im-plor-ing cry, "Forgive, they know not what they do!"
Nor saw Thee in that "upper room," Nor met Thee on the o-pen way;
Who raised to heaven their wond'ring view, Then low to earth all prostrate bend;

CHORUS.

But we believe Thy footsteps trod Its streets and plains, Thou Son of God;
But we believe the deed was done, That shook the earth and veiled the sun;
But we believe that angels said, "Why seek the living with the dead?"
But we believe that human eyes Be-held that journey to the skies;

Ritard.

But we believe Thy footsteps trod Its streets and plains, Thou Son of God.
But we believe the deed was done, That shook the earth and veiled the sun.
But we believe that angels said, "Why seek the living with the dead?"
But we believe that human eyes Be-held that journey to the skies.

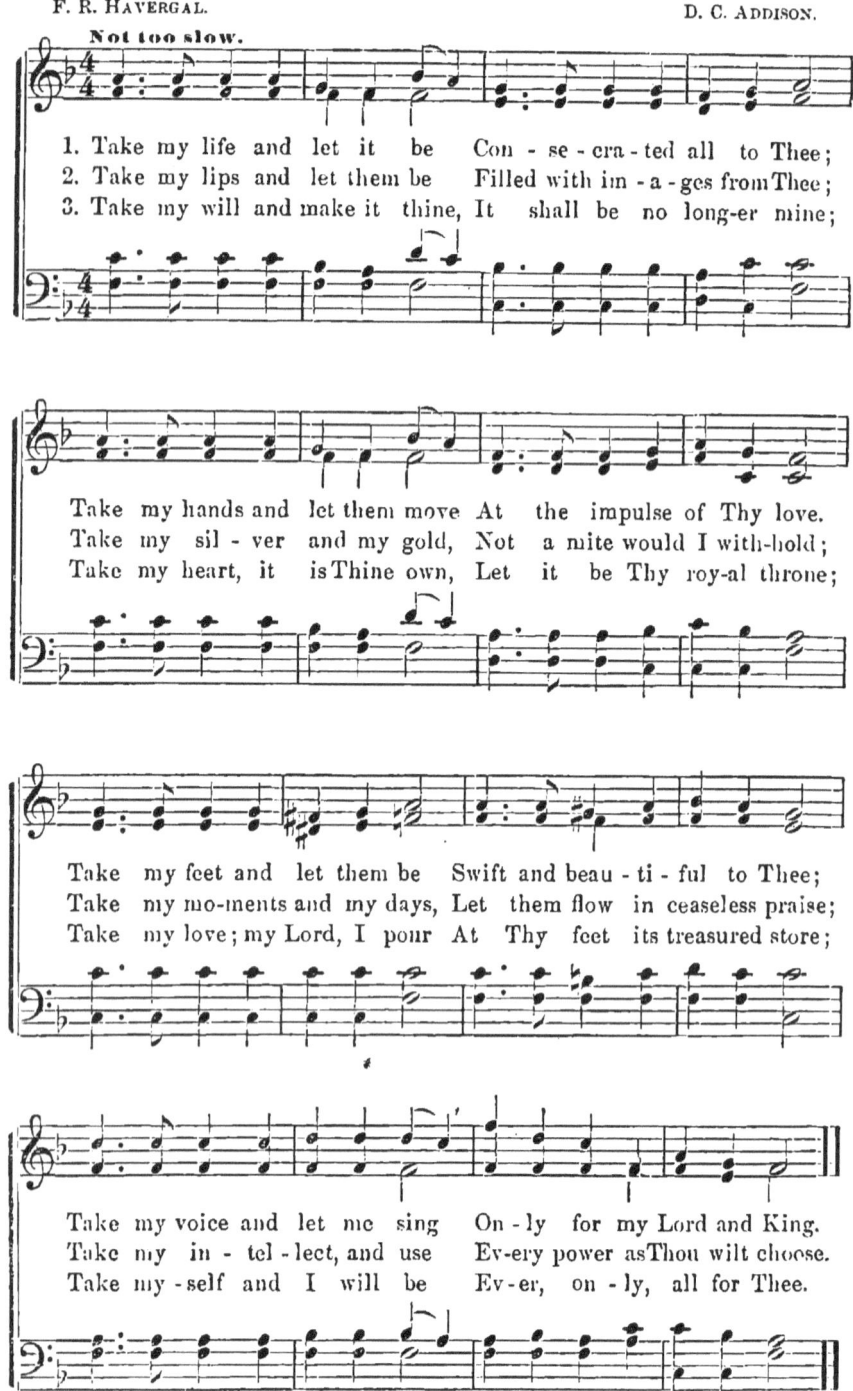

No. 16. BE IN OUR MIDST TO-DAY.

GRACE GLENN.   J. H. F.

1. We haste to Thy temple, oh, Father! We long for Thy presence to-day;
2. We haste to Thy temple, oh, Father! Our fast fading strength to re-new;
3. We haste to Thy temple, dear Father, Smile down from Thy glory a-bove;

As thirst panting harts by the way-side De-light by the waters to stray.
Bind up thou the wounded in spir-it, Our faith and our courage re-new.
We shall not grow weary well-doing, If blest by Thy presence of love.

CHORUS.

Greet with Thy presence Thy children, Lord, Grant us the promise of Thy word;
Je-sus, we need Thee on our way, Be in our midst to-day.

By per. FILLMORE BROS. From "Songs of Gratitude."

SINGING FOR JESUS. Concluded.

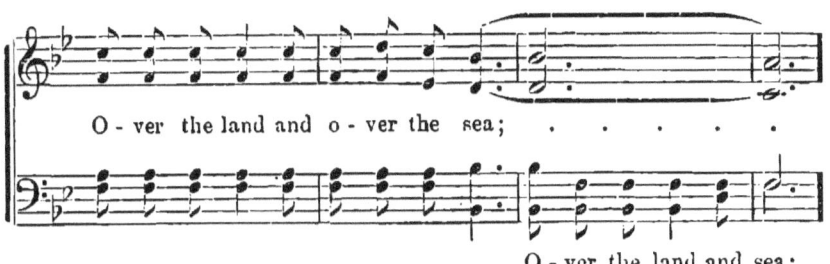

O-ver the land and o-ver the sea;
O-ver the land and sea;

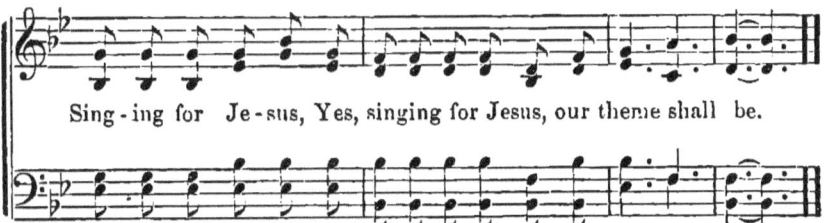

Sing-ing for Je-sus, Yes, singing for Jesus, our theme shall be.

No. 18.   MY GRACIOUS REDEEMER.

1. My gracious Re-deem-er I love, His praises aloud I'll proclaim,
   And join with the ar-mies a-bove, To shout His a-dor-able name.
D.C. And feel them in-cessant-ly shine, My boundless, in-ef-fa-ble joy.

2. You pal-aces, scepters and crowns, Your pride with disdain I survey,
   Your pomps are but shadows and sounds, And pass in a moment a-way.
D.C. My joy ev-er-last-ing-ly flows, My God, my Redeemer, is mine.

To gaze on His glo-ries di-vine, Shall be my e-ternal em-ploy,
The crown that my Savior be-stows, Yon permanent sun shall outshine;

No. 20. TO-DAY THE SAVIOR CALLS.

1. To-day the Savior calls; Ye, wan-d'rers come;
2. To-day the Savior calls; Oh, hear Him now!
3. To-day the Savior calls; For refuge fly;
4. The Spirit calls to-day; Yield to His power;

Oh, ye benighted souls, Why longer roam?
Within these sacred walls To Jesus bow.
The storm of justice falls, And death is nigh.
Oh, grieve Him not away, 'Tis mercy's hour.

No. 21. WILL YOU GO?

1. We're trav'ling home to heaven above, Will you go? will you go?
   To sing the Savior's dying love, Will you go? will you go?
   D.C. And millions more are on the road, Will you go? will you go?

2. We're going to see the bleeding Lamb, Will you go? will you go?
   In rapturous strains to praise His name, Will you go? will you go?
   D.C. And all the joys of heaven we'll share, Will you go? will you go?

Millions have reached that blest abode, Anointed kings and priests to God,
The crown of life we there shall wear, The conqueror's palms our hands shall bear,

No. 22. IF, LORD, THOU CALLEST ME.

"I am ready not to be bound only, but also to die for the name of the Lord."—Acts 21: 13.

D. C. ADDISON.   KNOWLES SHAW.

1. If, Lord, Thou call-est me, Here, Lord, am I;
2. If to Geth-sem-a-ne, To scenes of woe,
3. Or, if to Cal-va-ry, Lead-ing the way,
4. And, when this life is o'er, Oh, blest re-pose!

Wher-e'er Thou bid'st me be, Thi-ther I fly;
Thou, Lord, e'er call-est me, Thi-ther I go;
Lord, if Thou call-est me, I will o-bey;
Up-ward to Thee I soar, From death who rose;

If to Thy feast to come, Rich with Thy presence there,
There, if Thou call-est me, I answer, "Here, am I!"
There by Thy cross to be, There by Thy cross to die,
Lord, when Thou call-est me, Up-ward to Thee on high,

With wed-ding gar-ment on I will ap-pear.
Wher-e'er Thou send-est me, There would I fly.
If, Lord, Thou call-est me, "Here, Lord, am I."
"I come, I come to Thee," Bliss-ful my cry.

No. 25.   TARRY WITH ME.

"*And he went in to tarry with them.*"—Luke xxiv: 29.

KNOWLES SHAW.

1. Tar-ry with me, oh, my Sav-ior, For the day is passing by;
2. Many friends were gathered round me, In the bright days of the past;
3. Deeper, deep-er grow the shadows, Pa-ler now the glowing west;
4. Tar-ry with me, oh, my Sav-ior, Lay my head up-on Thy breast

See, the shades of evening gather, And the night is drawing nigh.
But the grave has closed above them, And I lin-ger here at last.
Swift the night of death ad-vances; Shall it be the night of rest?
Till the morning; then a-wake me, Morning of e-ter-nal rest.

CHORUS.

Tar-ry with me, blessed Je-sus, Leave me not till morning light;

For I'm lone-ly here without thee, Tar-ry with me thro' the night.

By permission of JOHN CHURCH & Co., owners of copyright.

WANDERING AWAY. Concluded.

Hear His gentle voice, Calling you to-day, And wander no more away from Jesus.

No. 29. WHEN SHALL WE MEET AGAIN?

DR. L. MASON.

1. When shall we meet a-gain, Meet ne'er to sev-er? When will peace
2. When shall love freely flow, Pure as life's riv-er? When shall sweet
3. Up to that world of light, Take us, dear Sav-ior; May we all

wreath her chain Round us for-ev-er? Our hearts will ne'er repose Safe
friendship glow, Changeless for-ev-er? Where joys ce-lestial thrill, Where
there u-nite, Hap-py for-ev-er: Where kindred spirits dwell, There

from each blast that blows, In this dark vale of woes—Never—no, never!
bliss each heart shall fill, And fears of parting chill, Never—no, never!
may our music swell, And time our joys dispel, Never—no, never!

No. 32. ANY MAY COME.

"Come unto me, all ye that labor and are heavy laden, and I will give you rest."—Matt. 11: 28.

E. R. Latta.   Knowles Shaw.

1. A-ny may come to Je-sus, Who was for sin-ners slain;
2. A-ny may come to Je-sus; Who will the call o-bey?
3. A-ny may come to Je-sus; Oh, what a bless-ed thought!

And if they rightly will seek Him, They shall not seek in vain.
Say, will you trusting approach Him? He will not turn a-way.
Come from our sin-ful bond-age, He has our free-dom bought.

A-ny may claim His prom-ise, A-ny may taste His love;
Oh, what a blest as-sur-ance, When we are sore op-prest;
Not for the few He suffered, Not for the few His call;

A-ny who faith-ful-ly serve Him, Rest in His arms a-bove.
On-ly to know that the Sav-ior, Free-ly will give you rest.
Death for the world He has tasted, Par-don is free for all.

Chorus.

A-ny may come, "free-ly come;" Come to this lov-ing Je-sus;

ANY MAY COME. Concluded.

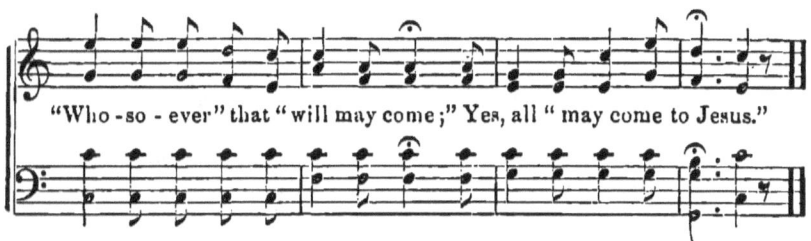

"Who-so-ever" that "will may come;" Yes, all " may come to Jesus."

No. 33.   JOY TO THE WORLD.

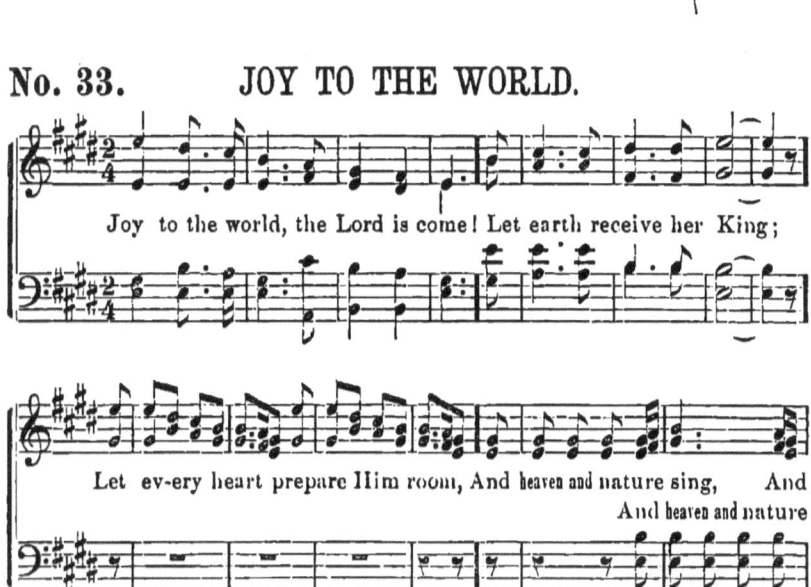

Joy to the world, the Lord is come! Let earth receive her King;
Let ev-ery heart prepare Him room, And heaven and nature sing, And
heaven and nature sing, And heaven, And heaven and na-ture sing.

2 Joy to the earth, the Savior reigns!
   Let men their songs employ;
   While fields and floods, rocks, hills, and plains,
   Repeat the sounding joy.

3 No more let sins and sorrows grow,
   Nor thorns infest the ground;
   He comes to make His blessings flow
   Far as the curse is found.

4 He rules the world with truth and grace,
   And makes the nations prove
   The glories of His righteousness,
   And wonders of His love.

I NEED THEE, PRECIOUS JESUS. Concluded.

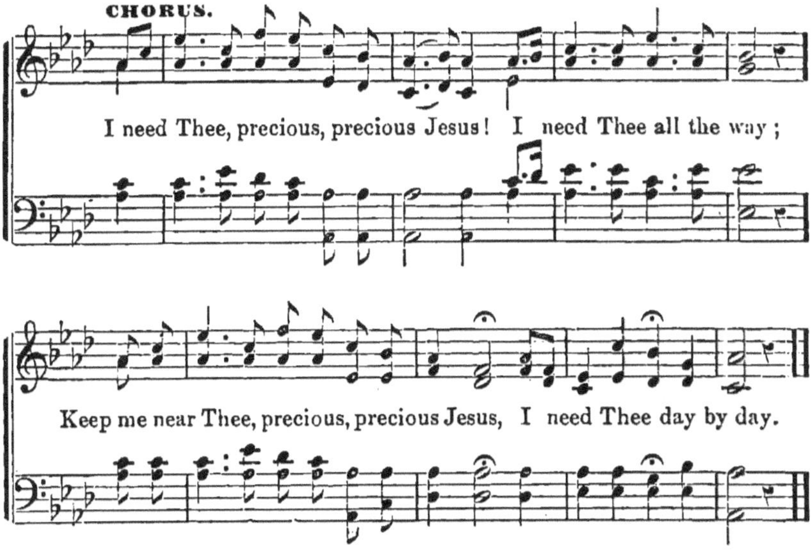

CHORUS.

I need Thee, precious, precious Jesus! I need Thee all the way;

Keep me near Thee, precious, precious Jesus, I need Thee day by day.

No. 35. MY SOUL, BE ON THY GUARD.

DR. L. MASON.

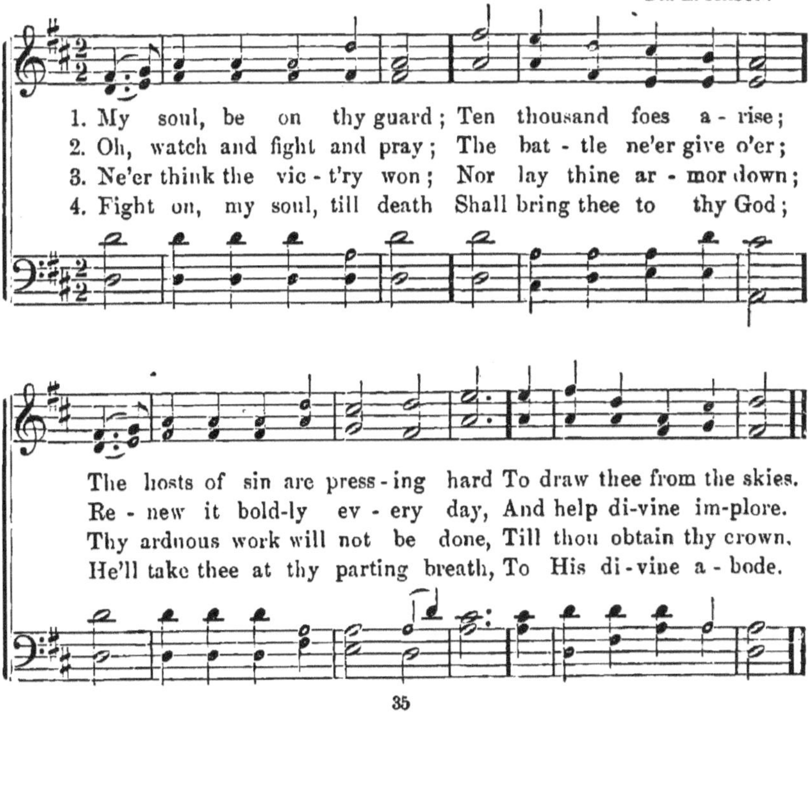

1. My soul, be on thy guard; Ten thousand foes a-rise;
2. Oh, watch and fight and pray; The bat-tle ne'er give o'er;
3. Ne'er think the vic-t'ry won; Nor lay thine ar-mor down;
4. Fight on, my soul, till death Shall bring thee to thy God;

The hosts of sin are press-ing hard To draw thee from the skies.
Re-new it bold-ly ev-ery day, And help di-vine im-plore.
Thy arduous work will not be done, Till thou obtain thy crown.
He'll take thee at thy parting breath, To His di-vine a-bode.

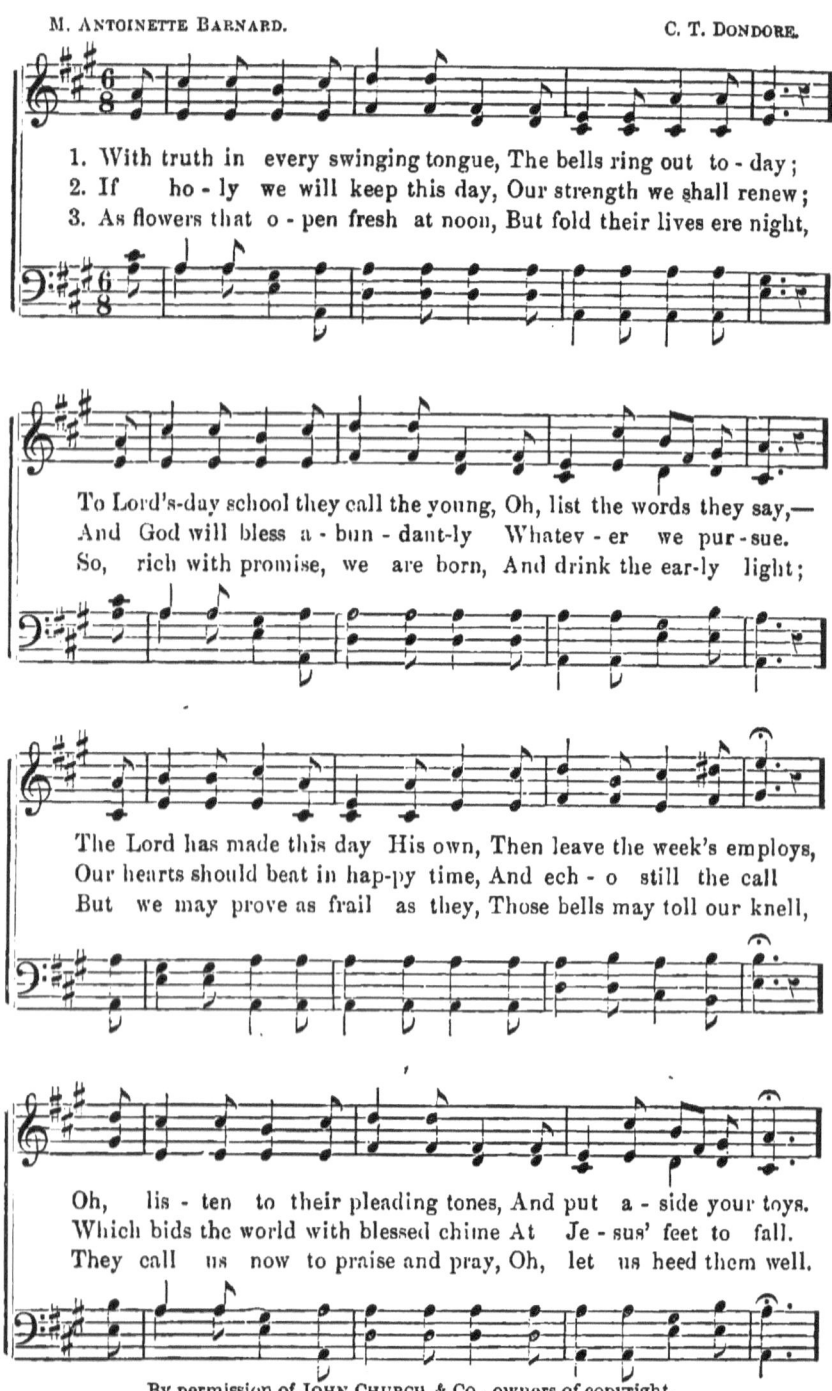

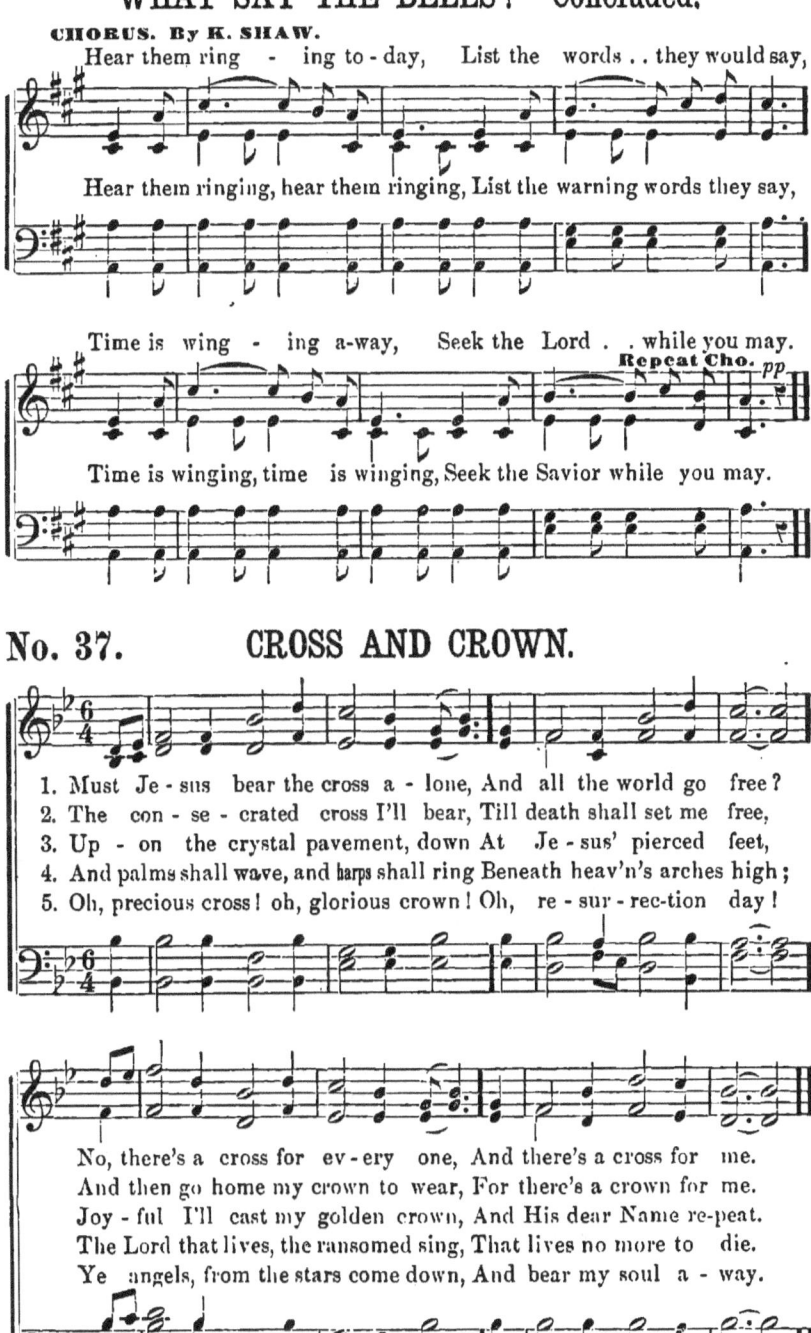

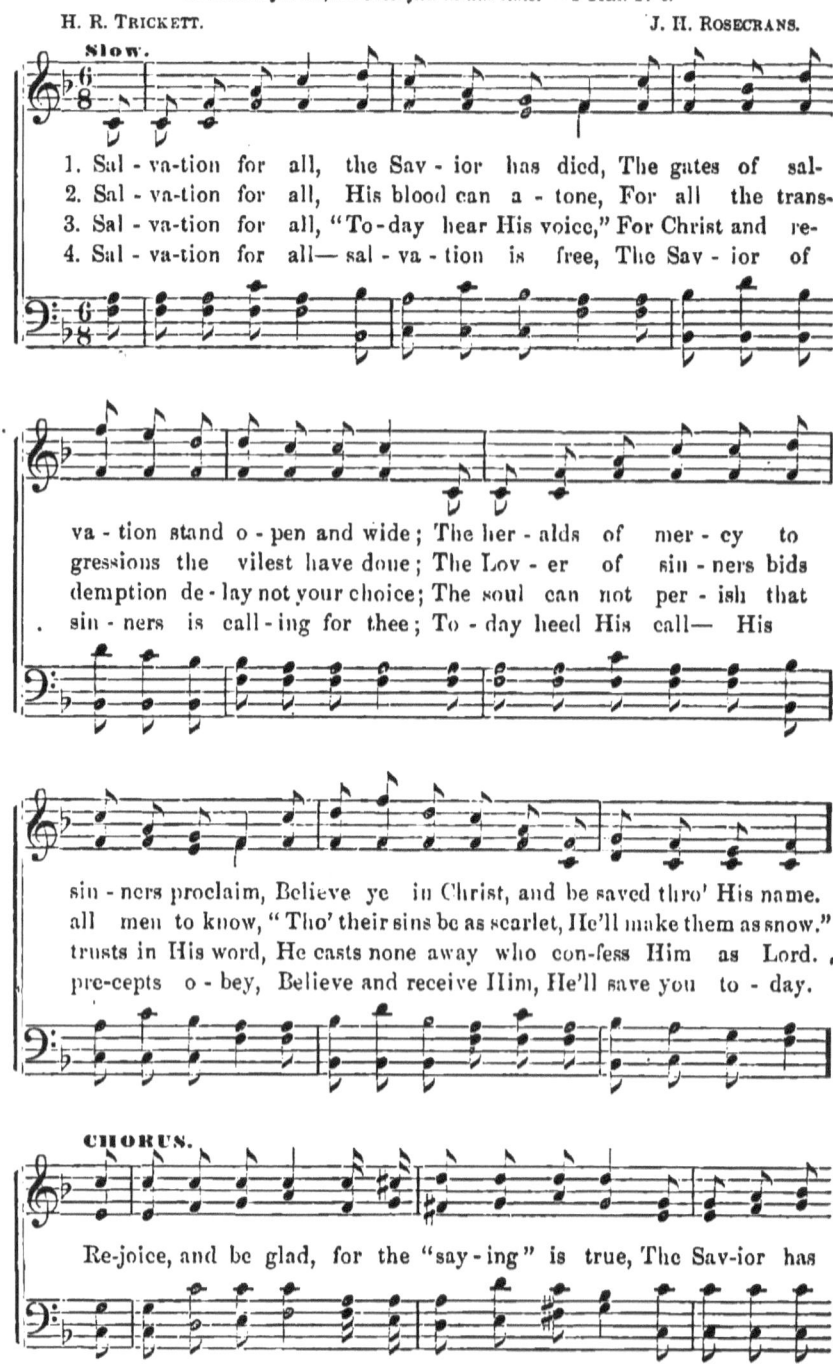

SALVATION FOR ALL. Concluded.

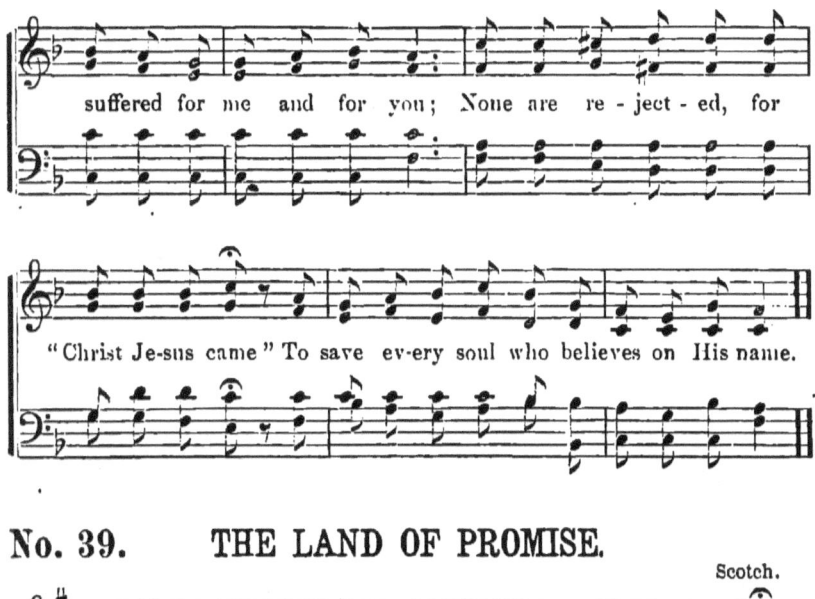

No. 39. THE LAND OF PROMISE.

Scotch.

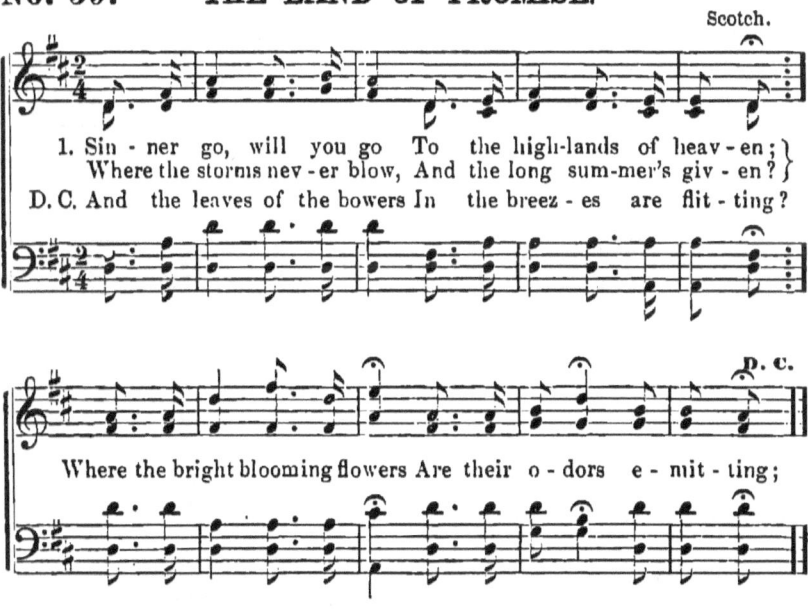

2 Where the rich golden fruit
　　Is in bright clusters pending,
　And the deep laden boughs
　　Of life's fair tree are bending;
　And where life's crystal stream
　　Is unceasingly flowing,
　And the verdure is green,
　　And eternally growing?

3 He's prepared thee a home—
　　Sinner, canst thou believe it?
　And invites thee to come—
　　Sinner, wilt thou receive it?
　Oh come, sinner, come,
　　For the tide is receding,
　And the Savior will soon,
　　And forever, cease pleading.

NOT FAR FROM THE KINGDOM. Concluded.

king-dom of God; .... Not far, ... Not
king-dom, the king-dom of God; Not far from the kingdom, Not
far, ... Not far from the kingdom of God.
far from the kingdom, Not far from the kingdom of God.

No. 41. LOVE FOR ALL.

WARTENSEE.

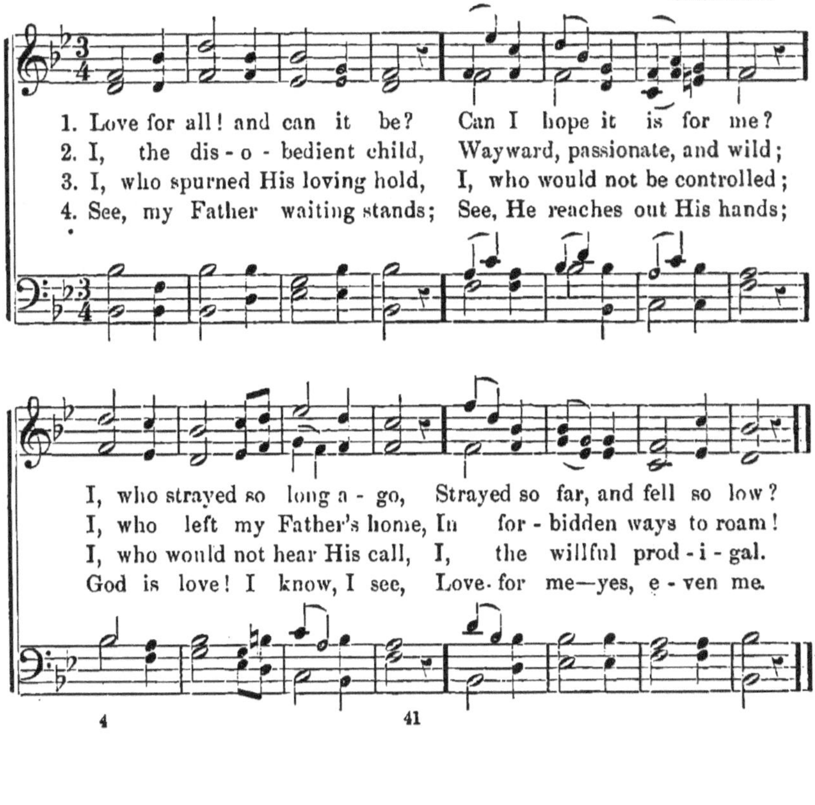

1. Love for all! and can it be?   Can I hope it is for me?
2. I, the dis-o-bedient child,   Wayward, passionate, and wild;
3. I, who spurned His loving hold,   I, who would not be controlled;
4. See, my Father waiting stands;   See, He reaches out His hands;

I, who strayed so long a-go,   Strayed so far, and fell so low?
I, who left my Father's home,   In for-bidden ways to roam!
I, who would not hear His call,   I, the willful prod-i-gal.
God is love! I know, I see,   Love for me—yes, e-ven me.

No. 42. WHO SHALL BE ABLE TO STAND?

"For the great day of His wrath is come, and who shall be able to stand."—Rev. 6: 17.

K. SHAW.   KNOWLES SHAW.

1. When the trump of God shall sound, And the nations gather round, And the
2. When the deluge swept the world, And to death its millions hurl'd, And the
3. When the cities of the plain Were enveloped in the flame, And de-
4. When the day of wrath is come, And the day of mercy gone, And to

Judge shall sit upon His royal throne; Who will hear the welcome word,
wa - ters covered o - ver all the land; Those who trusted in the Lord,
struc - tion swept the mul-ti-tudes a - way; There was just a lit-tle band,
judgment they are called from every land; Sin-ner, how is it with thee?

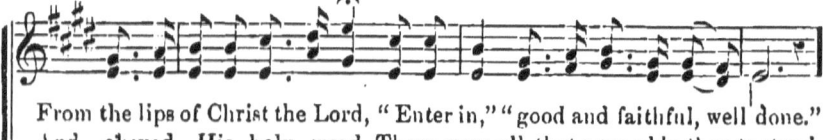

From the lips of Christ the Lord, "Enter in," "good and faithful, well done."
And obeyed His holy word, These were all that were able then to stand.
Who were able then to stand, In that great and that ter-ri - ble day.
Christian, how then shall it be? Shall we all be a-ble then to stand?

CHORUS.

Who shall be a - ble then to stand? Who shall be

Who shall be a - ble, shall be a - ble then to stand? Who shall be

WHO SHALL BE ABLE TO STAND? Concluded.

No. 43. NOT ASHAMED OF CHRIST.

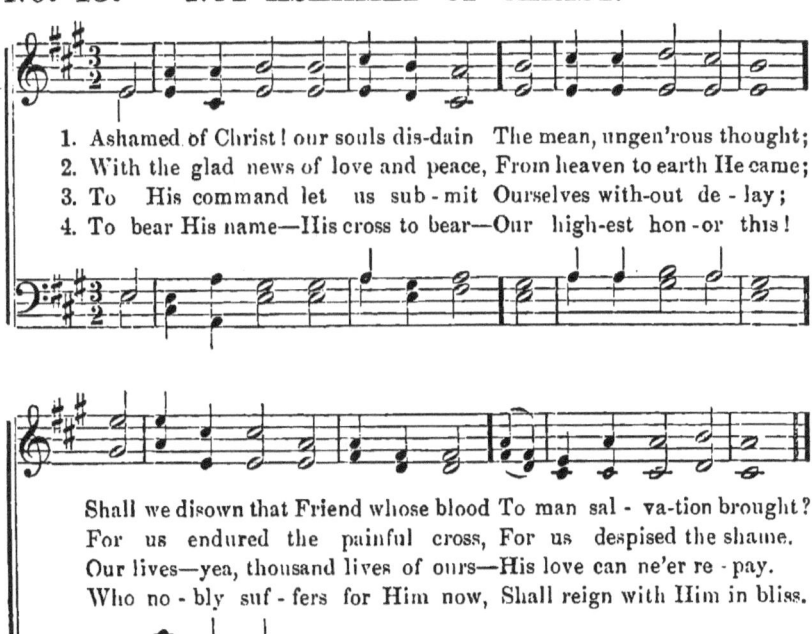

1. Ashamed of Christ! our souls disdain The mean, ungen'rous thought;
2. With the glad news of love and peace, From heaven to earth He came;
3. To His command let us submit Ourselves without delay;
4. To bear His name—His cross to bear—Our highest honor this!

Shall we disown that Friend whose blood To man salvation brought?
For us endured the painful cross, For us despised the shame.
Our lives—yea, thousand lives of ours—His love can ne'er repay.
Who nobly suffers for Him now, Shall reign with Him in bliss.

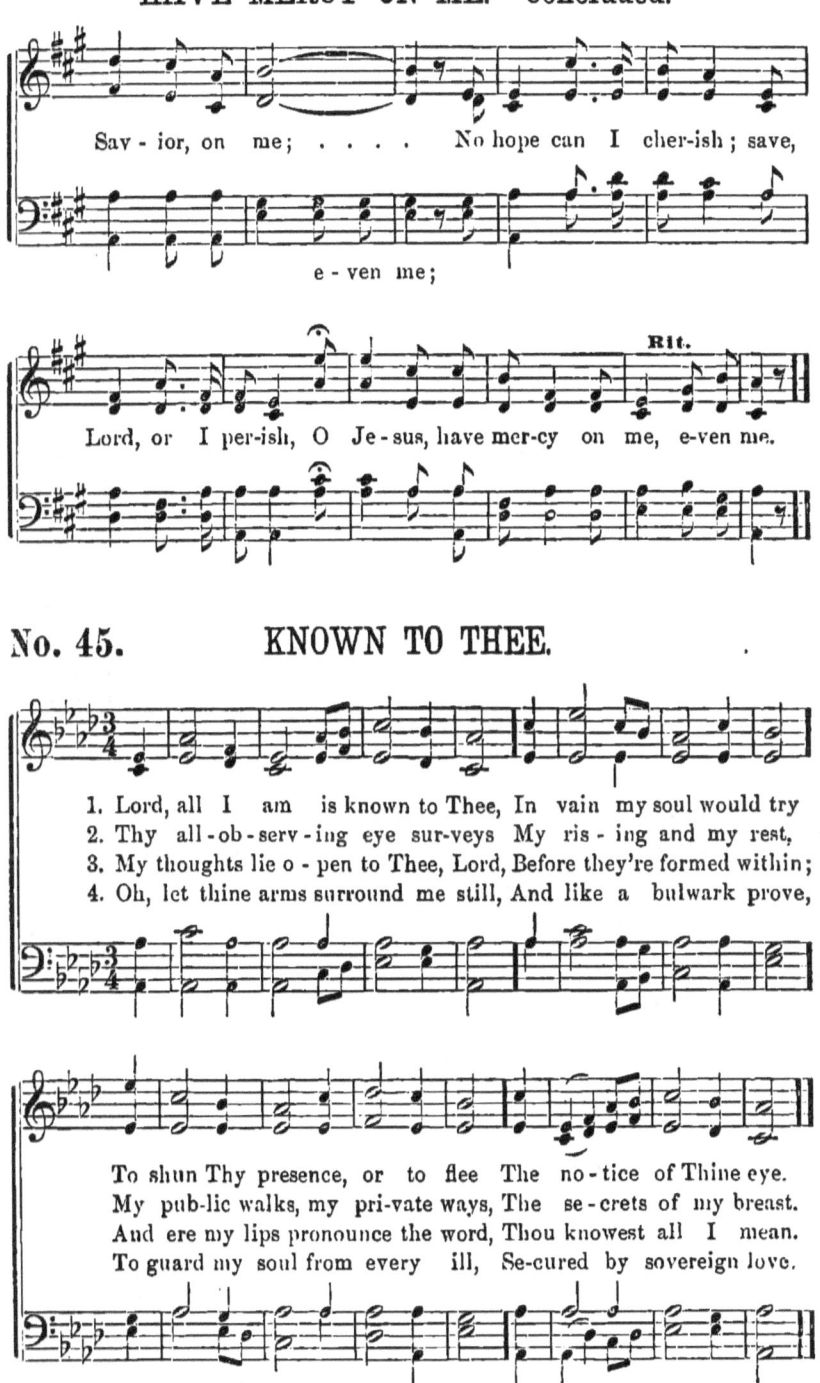

GO THY WAY FOR THIS TIME. Concluded.

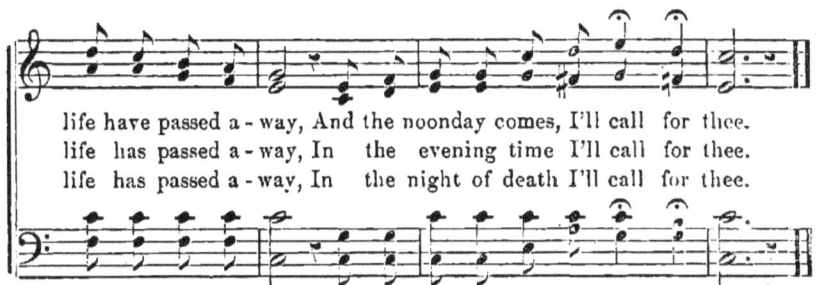

life have passed a-way, And the noonday comes, I'll call for thee.
life has passed a-way, In the evening time I'll call for thee.
life has passed a-way, In the night of death I'll call for thee.

No. 47. I LOVE THY KINGDOM, LORD.

1. I love Thy kingdom, Lord! The house of Thine abode, The church our blest Redeemer saved With His own precious blood. I love Thy church, O God! Her walls before Thee stand Dear as the apple of Thine eye, And graven on Thy hand.

2 For her my tears shall fall,
  For her my prayers ascend;
To her my cares and toils be given,
  Till toils and cares shall end.
Beyond my highest joy
  I prize her heavenly ways,
Her sweet communion, solemn vows,
  Her hymns of love and praise.

3 Jesus, Thou Friend divine,
  Our Savior and our King!
Thy hand from every snare and foe
  Shall great deliverance bring.
Sure as Thy truth shall last,
  To Zion shall be given
The brightest glories earth can yield,
  And brighter bliss of heaven.

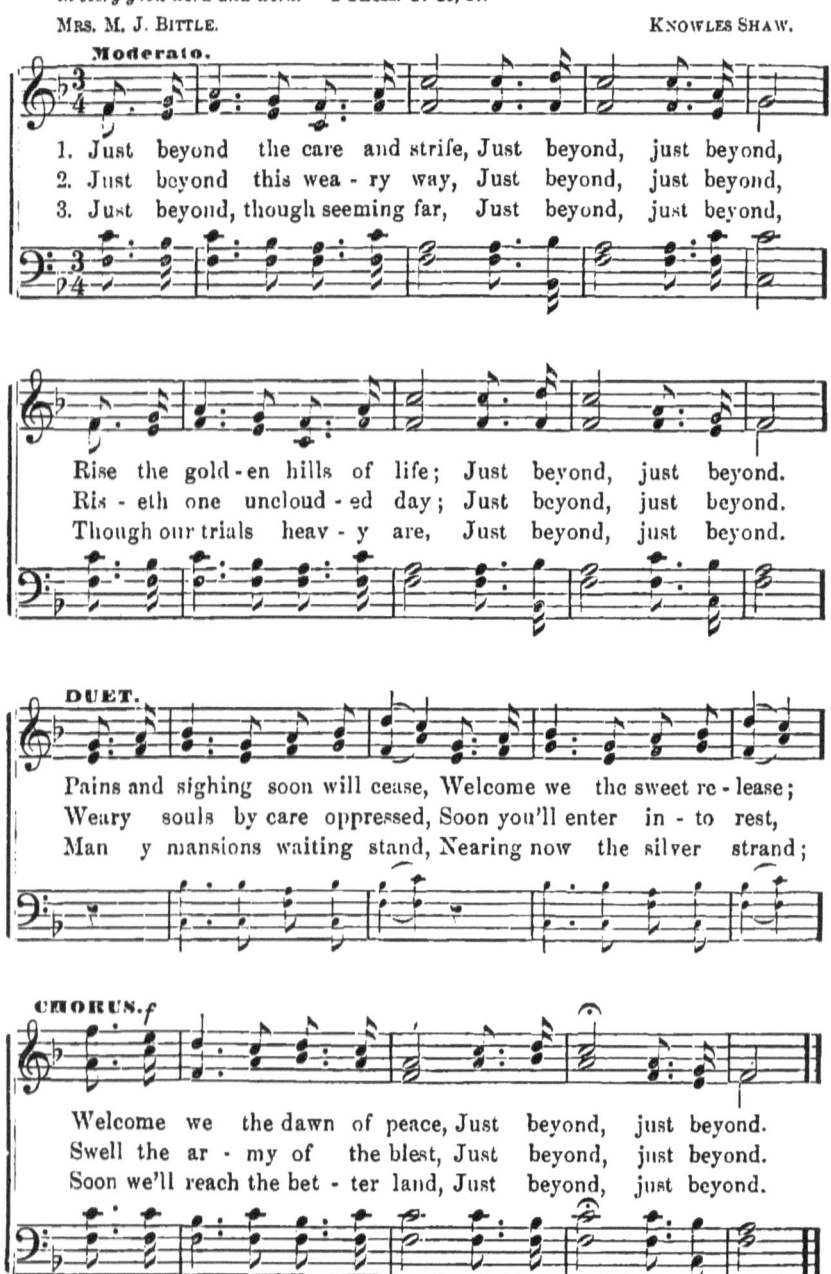

No. 49. A KINGDOM IN GLORY FOR ME.

" I go to prepare a place for you."—John 14: 2.

K. SHAW.   KNOWLES SHAW.

1. The Savior was mocked and His crown was of thorns, Yet a kingdom in glory had He; He shall sit on His throne in heaven above;—Oh, is that bright kingdom for me?
2. He reigns in the hearts of His people below, His scepter is peace all divine; He conquers His foes by the power of His love;—Oh, say, shall that kingdom be mine? There's a kingdom in glory for me, . . .
3. Yes, Jesus is King, and forever shall reign, Yet His kingdom is not of this world; To Him let us bow, His praise let us sing; His banner be ever unfurled.

CHORUS. Cheerfully.

A kingdom in glory for me, . . . A kingdom of peace while I
in glory for me,

No. 50. A HOME WITH JESUS.

"And so shall we be ever with the Lord."—1 Thess. 4: 17.

K. SHAW. KNOWLES SHAW.

1. A home with Jesus, my Sav-ior, Who died on the cross for me;
2. We have but a glimpse of that mansion, While pilgrims we walk be-low;
3. Here hearts once united are severed, Here partings and tears ob-tain;

To dwell in His kingdom forever, For-ever with Jesus to be.
To that home where the dear ones shall gather, That kingdom where Christians shall go.
But all who are true to the Savior, Shall meet on that heavenly plain.

To reign with the Savior in glo-ry, When all our wanderings cease;
But sweet is the stream ever flowing, From the fountain of joy over there;
Oh, sweet is this glo-ri-ous prospect, That we from all pain shall be free;

He has gone to prepare me a mansion, A home and a kingdom of peace.
Blessed Savior, each day, oh, prepare me, That rest and that mansion to share.
The hope of a blest re-sur-rec-tion, For-ev-er with Jesus to be.

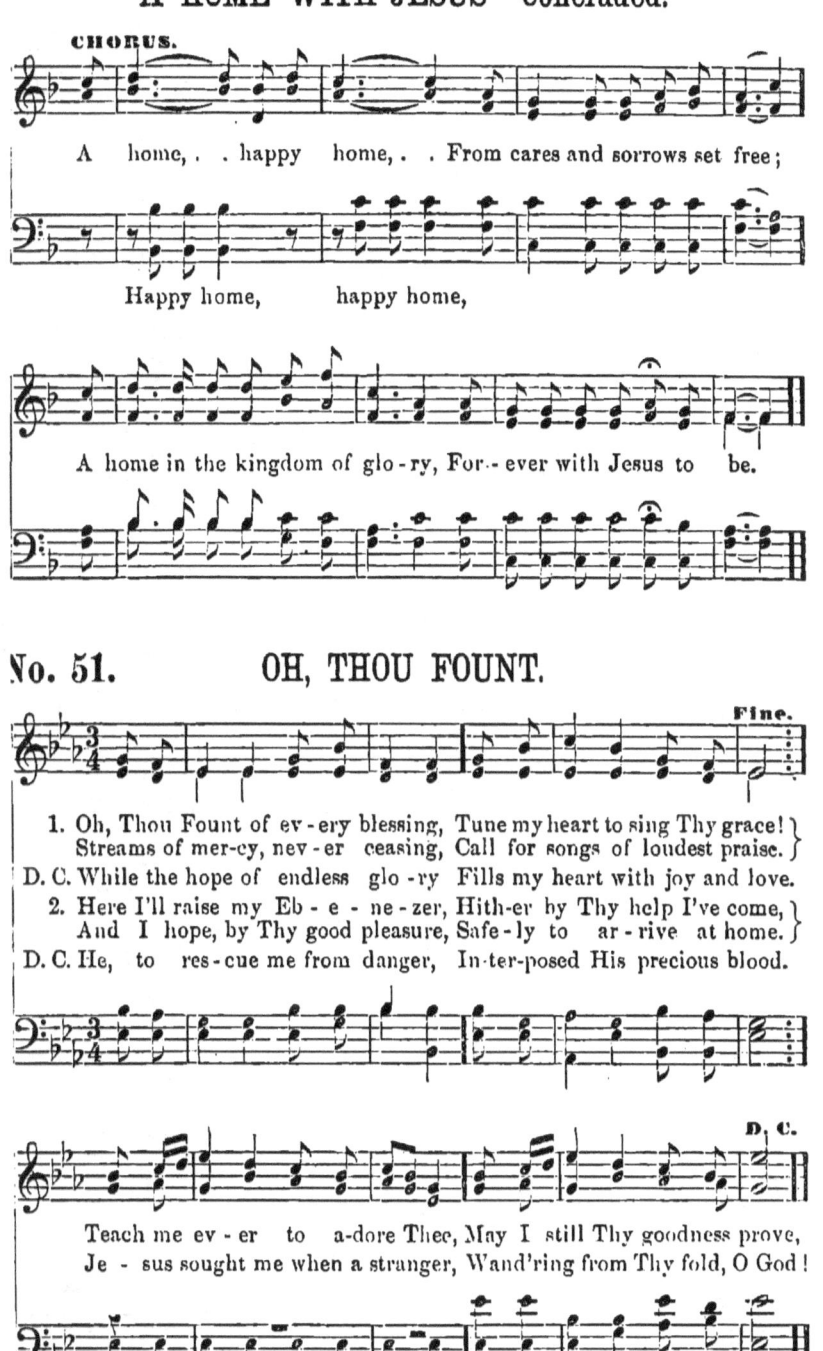

No. 52. BEAUTIFUL DREAM.

KNOWLES SHAW. KNOWLES SHAW.

1. I dreamed of the land of the pure and bright, The cit-y of God, the saint's de-light, And the saints of all ag-es and children were there, That cit-y of God and that home to share.
2. I dreamed that the tri-als of life were o'er, And the saints were walking the golden shore; Where they ate of the fruit of life's ev-er-green tree, O! beauti-ful, beau-ti-ful dream to me.
3. I dreamed that I saw them in robes of white; With crowns on their brow of gold-en light; I looked as they wandered life's riv-er a-long, I listened and heard a most beau-ti-ful song.

CHORUS.

O! that beautiful dream; O! that beautiful dream; Beautiful dream. Beautiful dream. Shall I the saints, and those children see, Or, shall it be on-ly a dream?

By permission of JOHN CHURCH & Co., owners of copyright.

No. 54. THE OTHER LAND.

MRS. A. L. DAVISON.   J. H. F.

1. Somewhere beyond the vis-ion Of our despairing eyes,
Within the land e-lys-ian, The hills of glo-ry rise;
2. And soft-ly, sweetly, flow-ing, A riv-er windeth fair,
Thro' all the gold-en glo-ry That reigns for-ev-er there;
3. When thro' the golden por-tal, At last we en-ter in,
Thro' him who hath re-deemed us, A fadeless crown we win;

REFRAIN.

What words can tell the beau-ty Of that ce-les-tial land,
And of those shining wa-ters, The dy-ing souls of men
And in that world of beau-ty, With all the ransomed throng,

The cit-y God hath build-ed By his al-might-y hand.
Shall drink with end-less rapt-ure, And, drinking, live a-gain.
We'll join with cease-less rapt-ure, The ev-er-last-ing song.

By per. FILLMORE BROS. From "Songs of Gratitude."

No. 56. WHEN THE COMFORTER COMES.

"He shall give you another Comforter."—John 14: 16.

K. SHAW.   KNOWLES SHAW.

1. The hearts of the Savior's dis-ci-ples were sad, He had said He was go-ing a-way; But the promise was sweet, "when the Com-fort-er comes, For-ever with you He will stay;" But the promise was sweet, "when the Comforter comes, For-ev-er with you He will stay."

2. Con-vinc-ing the world of its sin and its woe, And to speak of a man-sion a-bove; To tell how to Christ poor sin-ners may go, For pardon, for peace, and His love; To tell how to Christ poor sin-ners may go, For pardon, for peace, and His love.

3. If we're children of God, then His Spir-it He'll give, For our comfort while pilgrims be-low; Then like Him, and with Him, we ev-er shall live, When to that bright kingdom we go; Then like Him and with Him we ev-er shall live, When to that bright kingdom we go.

CHORUS.

"When the Com-fort-er comes," Oh, prom-ise so sweet; "When the

WHEN THE COMFORTER COMES. Concluded.

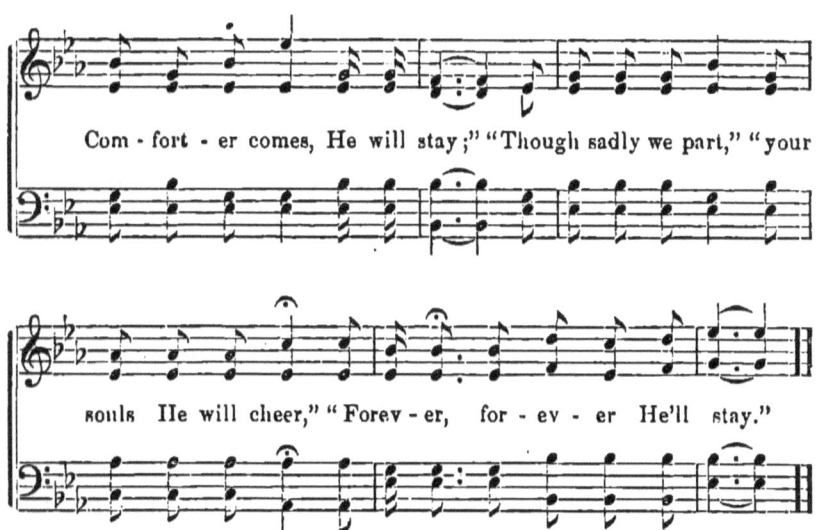

Com - fort - er comes, He will stay;" "Though sadly we part," "your souls He will cheer," "Forev - er, for - ev - er He'll stay."

No. 57. THE GOSPEL BANNER.

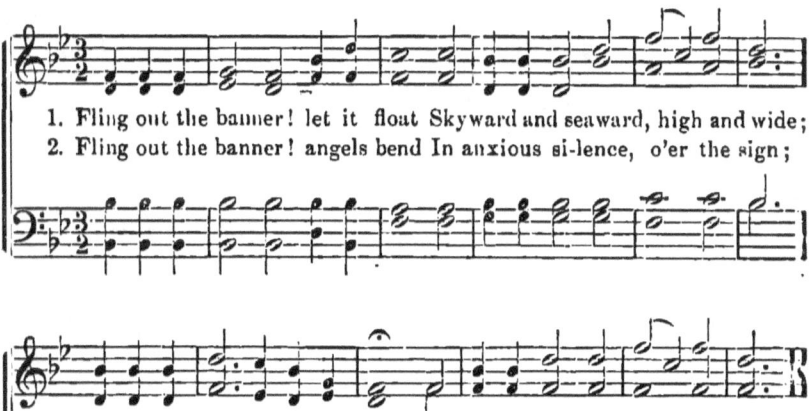

1. Fling out the banner! let it float Skyward and seaward, high and wide;
2. Fling out the banner! angels bend In anxious si-lence, o'er the sign;

The sun, that lights its shining folds, The cross, on which the Savior died.
And vainly seek to compre-hend The wonder of the love di-vine.

3 Fling out the banner! sin-sick souls,
  That sink and perish in the strife,
  Shall touch in faith its radiant hem,
  And spring immortal into life.

4 Fling out the banner! let it float
  Skyward and seaward, high and wide;
  Our glory, only in the cross;
  Our only hope, the Crucified.

No. 59. SHELTER OF SAFETY.

M. T. HAUGHEY.

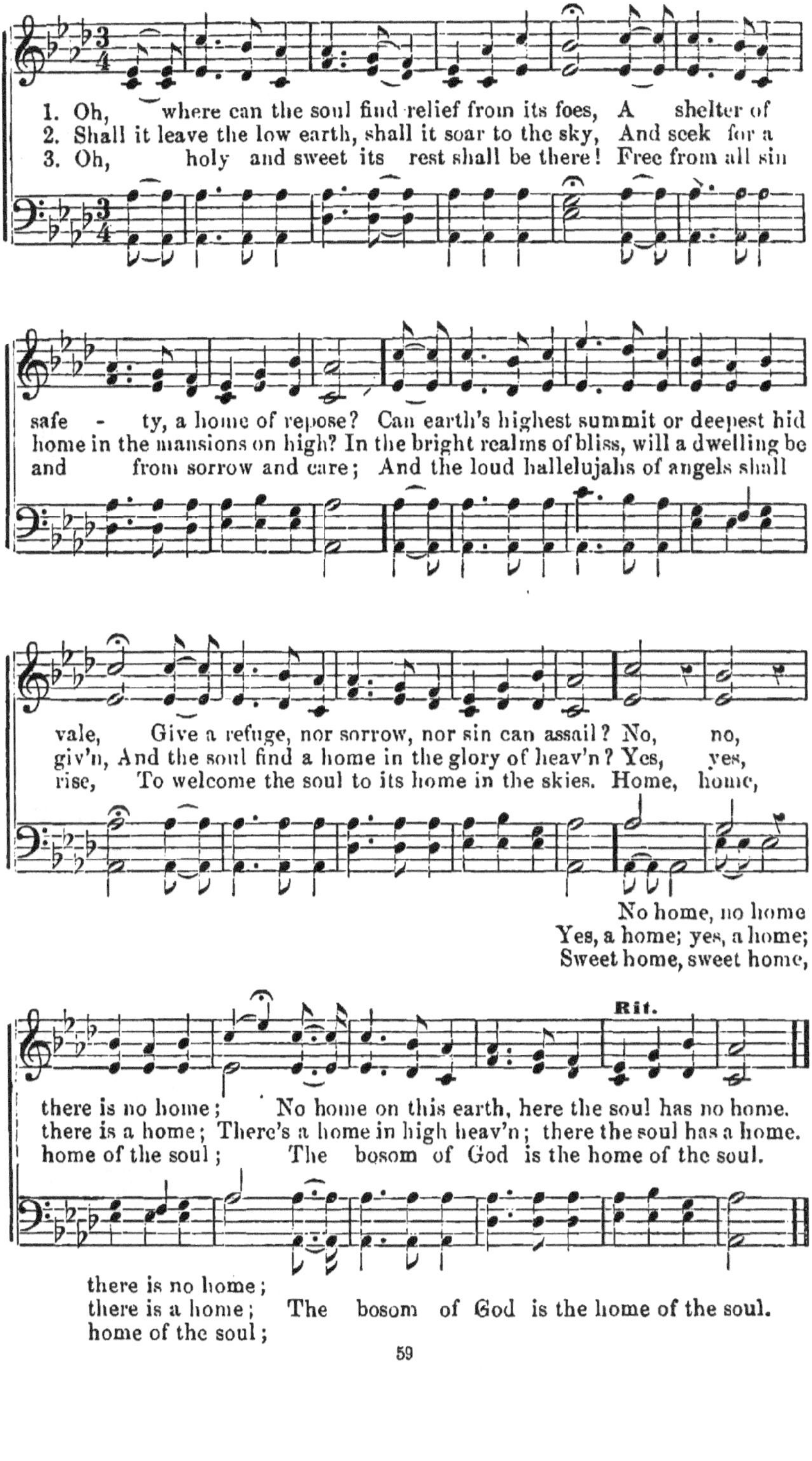

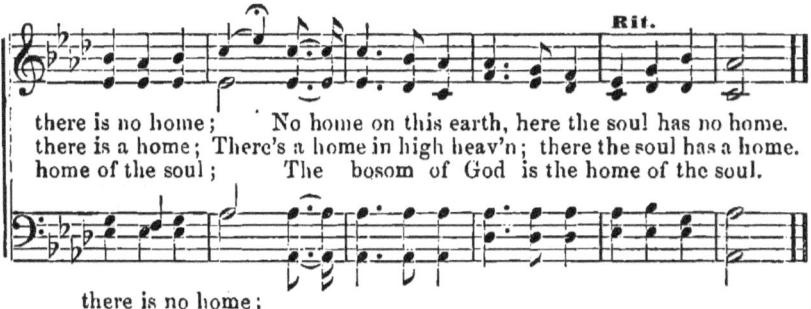

No. 63. THE SAVIOR IS COMING.

Read Isa. 11:9. Rev. 11:15. Ps. 20:5.

Mrs. M. B. C. Slade.   R. M. McIntosh.

1. From all the dark pla-ces Of earth's heathen ra-ces Oh, see how the thick shad-ows fly! The voice of sal-va-tion Awakes ev-ery na-tion, Come o-ver and help us, they cry.
2. The sun-light is glanc-ing O'er ar-mies ad-vanc-ing To con-quer the king-doms of sin, Our Lord shall possess them, His presence shall bless them, His beau-ty shall enter them in.
3. With shouting and singing, And ju-bi-lant ringing, Their arms of re-bell-ion cast down, At last ev-ery na-tion, The Lord of sal-va-tion Their King and Redeemer shall crown!

CHORUS.

The Savior is coming, Oh, tell ye the sto-ry, His ban-ner exalted shall be! The earth shall be full of his knowledge and glo-ry, As wa-ters that cover the sea!

From "The Gem," by permission of R. M. McIntosh.

"BY AND BY." Concluded.

come again, Roses will bloom again, Joy shall be mine again, by and by.
live again, Friends shall all meet again, We shall be happy then, by and by.

No. 65.   NEARER TO THEE.

"Though He be not far from every one of us."—Acts 17: 27.

DR. L. MASON.

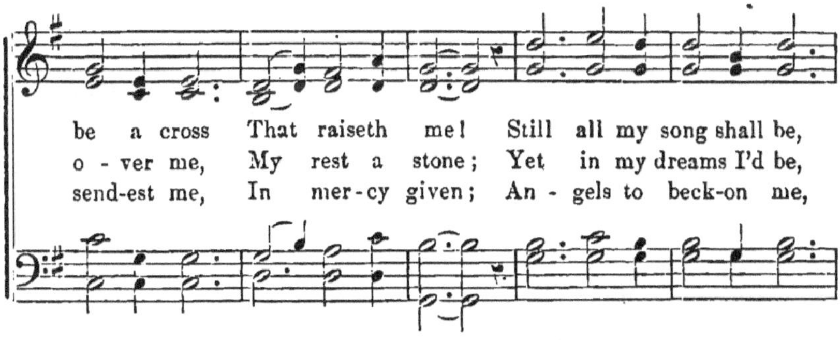

1. Near-er, my God, to Thee, Near-er to Thee! E'en tho' it be a cross That raiseth me! Still all my song shall be,
2. Tho' like the wan-der-er, The sun gone down, Dark-ness be o-ver me, My rest a stone; Yet in my dreams I'd be,
3. There let the way ap-pear Steps un-to heaven, All that Thou send-est me, In mer-cy given; An-gels to beck-on me,

Nearer, my God, to Thee, Nearer, my God, to Thee, Near-er to Thee!

No. 66. BEYOND THE DARK SEA.

"And so it came to pass that they all escaped safe to land."—Acts 27 : 44.

KNOWLES SHAW.

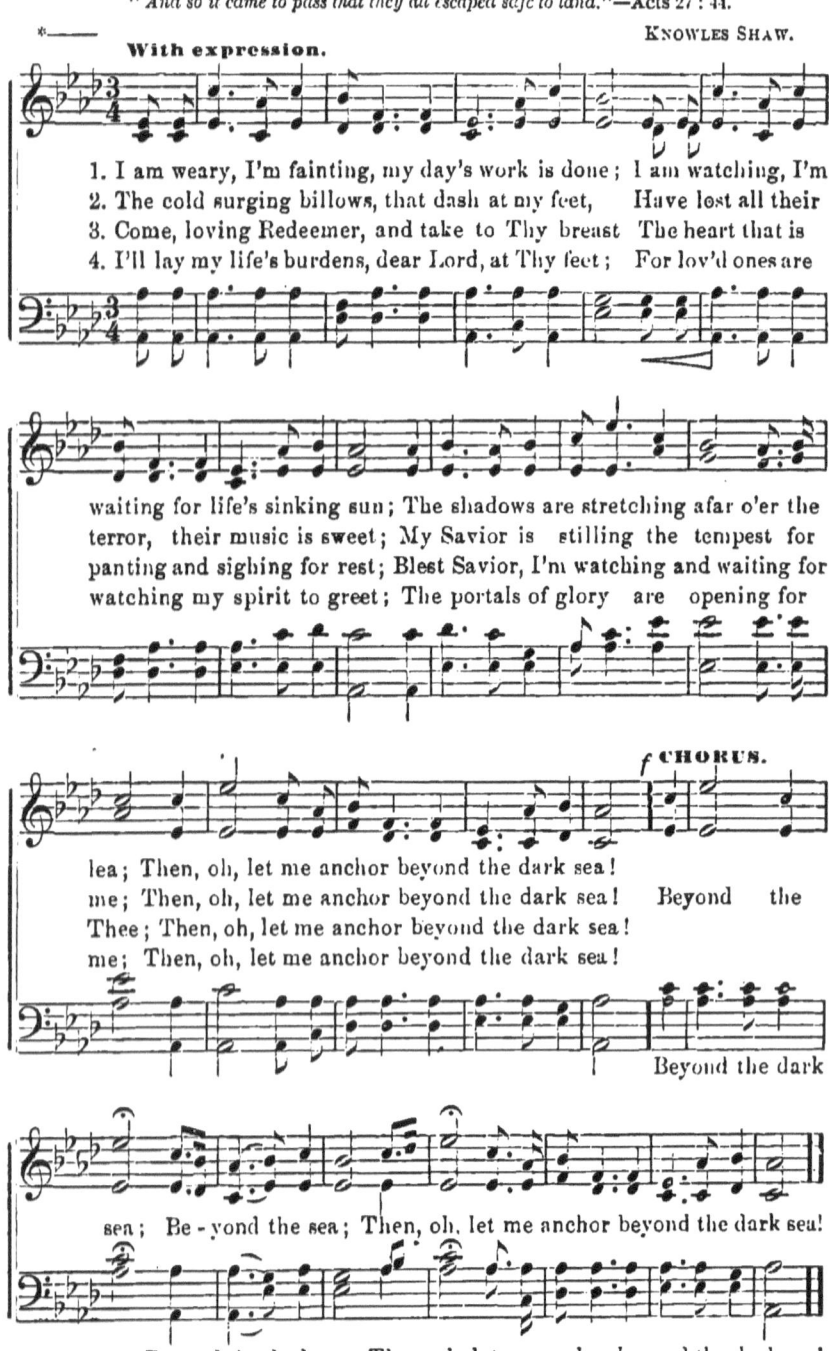

1. I am weary, I'm fainting, my day's work is done; I am watching, I'm waiting for life's sinking sun; The shadows are stretching afar o'er the lea; Then, oh, let me anchor beyond the dark sea!
2. The cold surging billows, that dash at my feet, Have lost all their terror, their music is sweet; My Savior is stilling the tempest for me; Then, oh, let me anchor beyond the dark sea!
3. Come, loving Redeemer, and take to Thy breast The heart that is panting and sighing for rest; Blest Savior, I'm watching and waiting for Thee; Then, oh, let me anchor beyond the dark sea!
4. I'll lay my life's burdens, dear Lord, at Thy feet; For lov'd ones are watching my spirit to greet; The portals of glory are opening for me; Then, oh, let me anchor beyond the dark sea!

CHORUS.

Beyond the dark sea; Beyond the sea; Then, oh, let me anchor beyond the dark sea!

No. 68. NOT MUCH FURTHER TO GO.

"The time of my departure is at hand."—2 Tim. 4: 6.

K. Shaw.   Knowles Shaw.

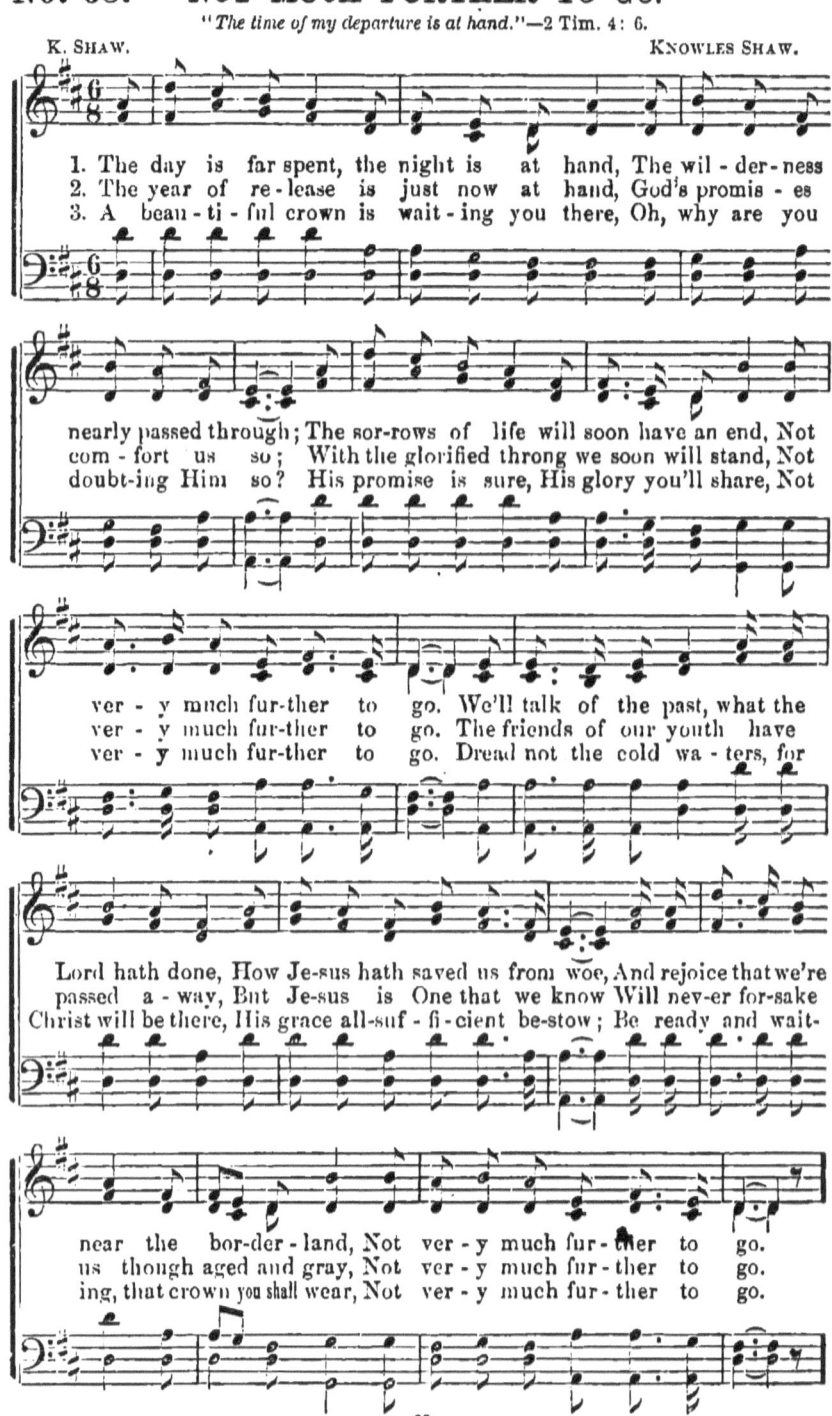

1. The day is far spent, the night is at hand, The wilderness nearly passed through; The sorrows of life will soon have an end, Not very much further to go. We'll talk of the past, what the Lord hath done, How Jesus hath saved us from woe, And rejoice that we're near the border-land, Not very much further to go.

2. The year of release is just now at hand, God's promises comfort us so; With the glorified throng we soon will stand, Not very much further to go. The friends of our youth have passed away, But Jesus is One that we know Will never forsake us though aged and gray, Not very much further to go.

3. A beautiful crown is waiting you there, Oh, why are you doubting Him so? His promise is sure, His glory you'll share, Not very much further to go. Dread not the cold waters, for Christ will be there, His grace all-sufficient bestow; Be ready and waiting, that crown you shall wear, Not very much further to go.

NOT MUCH FURTHER TO GO. Concluded.

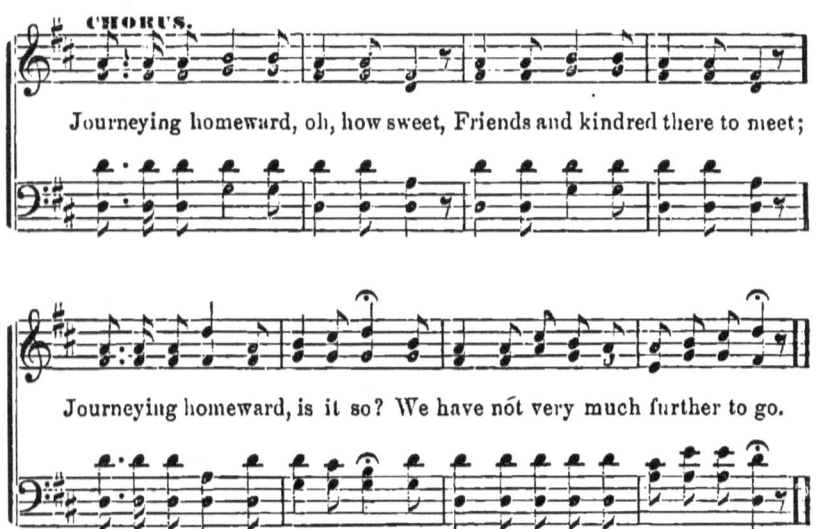

No. 69. SOUND THE TRUTH ABROAD.

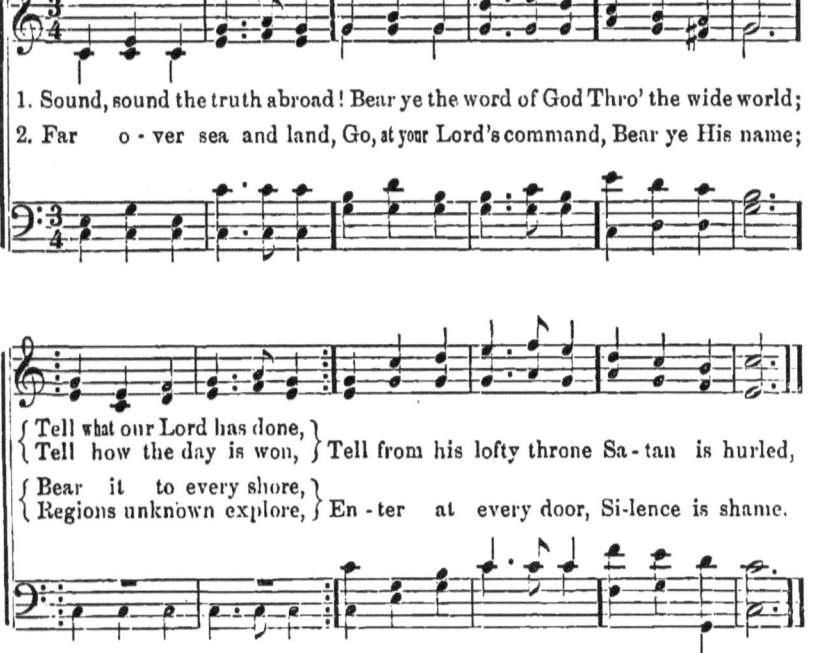

No. 71.   HEAVENLY MANSIONS.

"In my Father's house are many mansions."—John 14 : 2.

L. H. JAMESON.   KNOWLES SHAW.

1. There are mansions prepared in the skies, By the Savior who passed on before; And the Christian, whenever he dies, Finds a home where the saints die no more.
2. There the Father of Mercy a-bides, Whom the saints and the angels adore, And the river of life gently glides From His throne in that world ev-er-more.
3. There the Lamb that was slain ever lives In the light of the glory of God, And to all who obey Him He gives Robes made white in His own precious blood.

CHORUS.

Happy home, happy home, happy home, happy home, Happy home, where the saints die no more; Happy home, happy home, . . . Happy home, where the saints die no more.

No. 97.   "IF I WERE A VOICE."

KNOWLES SHAW.

SOLO. MELODY.

1. If I were a voice, a persuasive voice, That could travel this wide world
2. If I were a voice, a consoling voice, I would fly on the wings of the
3. If I were a voice, an immortal voice, That could travel this wide world

through; I would fly   on the beams of the morning light, I would
air;   The   homes   of sor-row and guilt I'd seek, And
round; Wher-ev-er   man to his idols bowed, I'd

speak to men with a gentle might, I'd tell them to be   true.
calm   and truth-ful words I'd speak, To save them from des-pair.
publish in notes both long and loud, The gos-pel's joy-ful sound.

I would fly, I would fly o-ver land and sea, Wher-ev-er a
I would fly, I would fly o'er the crowded town, I'd drop like the
I would fly, I would fly on the wings of day, Proclaiming peace

hu-man heart could be; Tell-ing a tale, or sing-ing a song, In
hap-py sunbeam down In-to the hearts of suf-fer-ing men, I'd
on my world-wide way; Bidding this saddened earth re-joice, If

CHORUS.

praise of the right, or in blame of the wrong.
teach them to look   up a-gain. I would fly, . . I would
I   were a voice, an im-mor-tal voice.

fly, I would fly, . . I would fly, I would fly over land and sea.

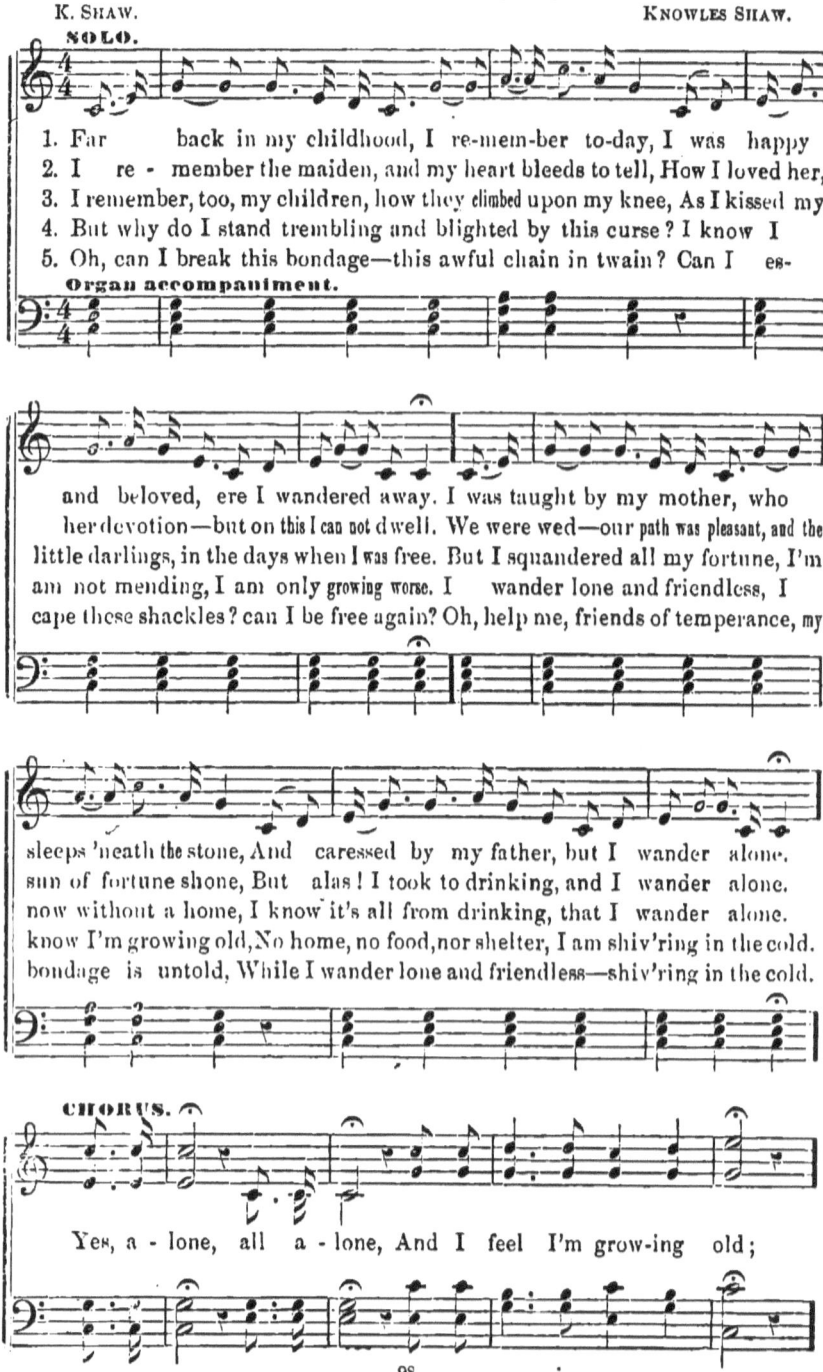

SHIVERING IN THE COLD. Concluded.

Yet I wan-der, oh, how lone-ly, I am shiv'ring in the cold.

No. 99. CHRIST, THE ONLY WAY.

"I am the way, the truth, and the life."—John 14: 6.

K. SHAW.   KNOWLES SHAW.

1. Sav-ior, Thou my way shall be, I will fol-low on-ly Thee;
2. Sav-ior, Thou my truth remain, On-ly Lamb for sin-ners slain!
3. Thou my life, my all shall be, Make me, Savior, more like Thee;

Be Thou near me night and day, Sav-ior, Thou, the on-ly way.
Take a-way my guilt, I pray, Sav-ior, Thou, the on-ly way.
Give me joy in end-less day, Sav-ior, Thou, the on-ly way.

CHORUS.   Rep. *pp*

Lead me on by night and day, Savior, Thou, the on-ly way.

SONG OF WELCOME. Concluded.

No. 105. "MY AIN COUNTRIE." Scotch Melody.

1. { I am far frae my hame, an' I'm weary aftenwhiles, For my
     An' I'll ne'er be fu' con-tent, un - til my een do see The
D. C. But these sichts an' these soun's will as naething be to me, When I

lang'd-for hame-bringing, an' my Father's welcome smiles,
gowden gates of heaven, an' my . . . . . ain countrie.
hear the angels sing-ing in my . . . . . ain countrie.

{ The earth is fleck'd with flowers, mony - tinted, fresh and gay;
  The bird-ies sing-ing blithely, for my Father made them sae; }

2 I've his gude word of promise that some gladsome day, the King
To His ain royal palace, His banished hame will bring.
Wi' een an' wi' heart flowing owre, we shall see
"The King in His beauty," in His ain countrie.
My sins hae been mony, an' my sorrows hae been sair:
But there they'll never vex me, nor be remembered mair:
His bluid hath made me white, an' His hand shall wipe my ee',
When He brings me hame at last to my ain countrie.

3 Like a bairn to its mither, a wee birdie to its nest,
I fain wad noo be ganging unto my Savior's breast,
For He gathers in His bosom, witless, worthless lambs like me,
He "carries them Himsel'," to His ain countrie.
He's faithfu' that has promised, He'll surely come again,
He'll keep His tryst wi' me, at what hour I dinna ken:
But He bids me still to wait, an' ready aye to be,
To gang at ony moment, to His ain countrie.

No. 106. "DRIFTING AWAY."

How many homes are made sad, by the dear ones drifting away.
"Wine is a mocker, and strong drink is raging."—Prov. 20: 1.

KNOWLES SHAW.

Not too fast.

1. Drift-ing a - part, drift-ing a,- part, Snapping the cords that are wound round the heart; Sun - der - ing ties that for - ev-er should be Firm ties for life, be - tween you and me. But oh, as I see you day af - ter day, I feel and I
2. Drift-ing a - way, drift-ing a - way, Drift-ing still fur - ther and fur - ther each day; Fur - ther and fur - ther out of my sight, Leav-ing me lone-ly—a - lone with the night. Yes, a - lone with the night, for e - ven the day Is changed in-to
3. Drift-ing a - part, drift-ing a - part, How sadly that feel-ing sinks in - to the heart; I thought that I had on this earth one friend, Faithful as truth, and true to the end. But oh, as I see you day af - ter day, I feel and I
4. Drift-ing a - way, drift-ing a - way, Drift-ing in si-lence, hence no one can say; But a prayer will be offered that one drift - ing bark, May nev-er drift into the un - known dark. But drift with its soul once worthy of love, In - to the wa-

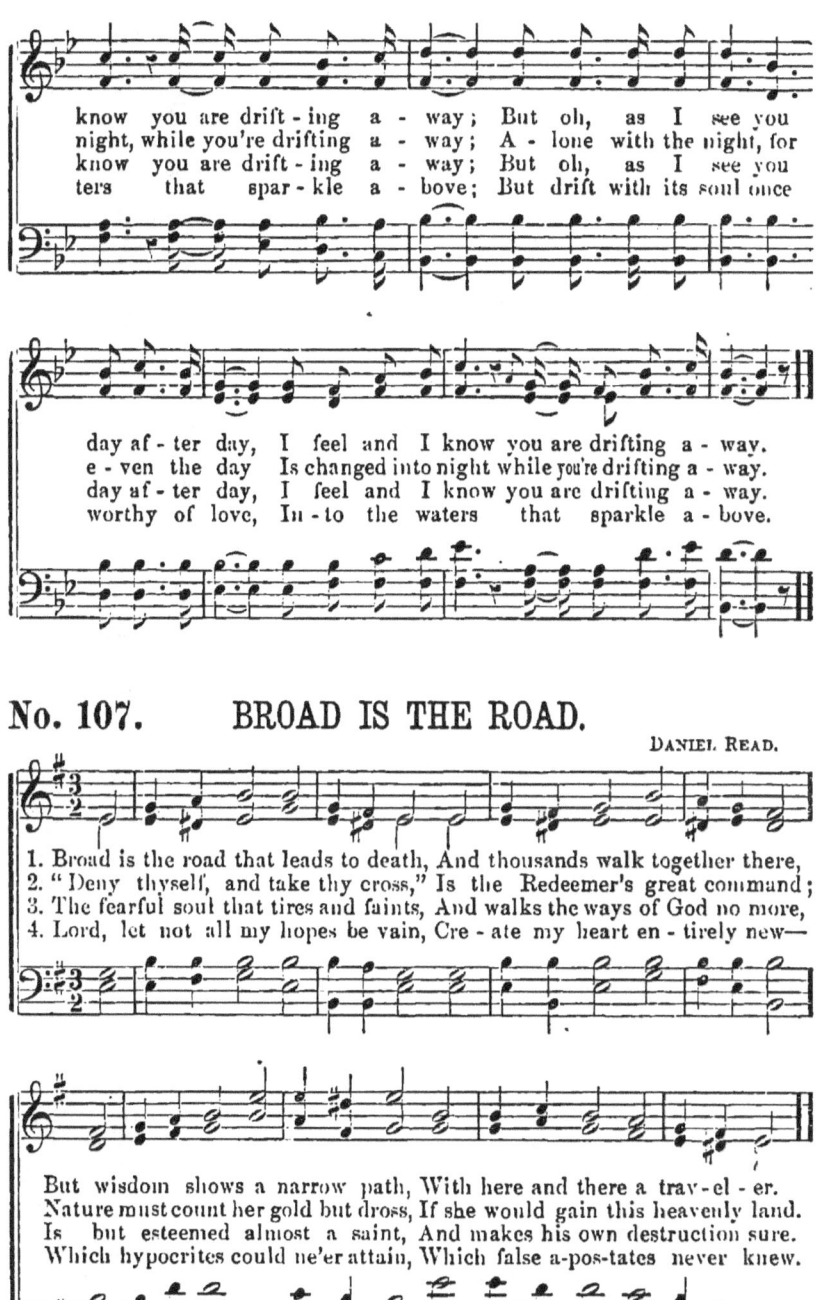

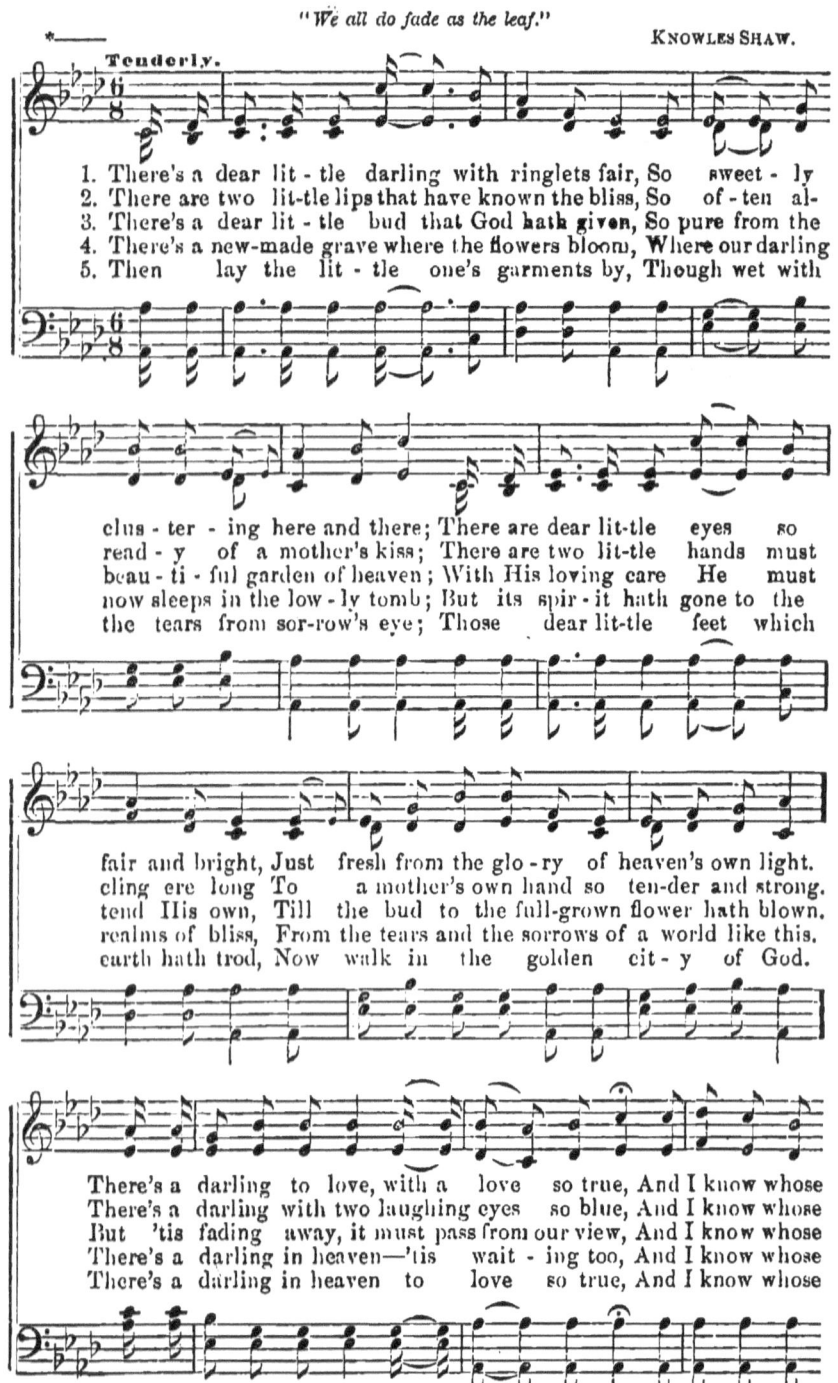

OUR DEAR LITTLE DARLING. Concluded.

darling that is—don't you? There's a dar-ling to love with a
darling that is—don't you? There's a dar-ling with two laughing
darling that is—don't you? But 'tis fad-ing a-way, it must
darling that is—don't you? There's a dar-ling in heaven—'tis
darling that is—don't you? There's a dar-ling in heaven to

love so true, And I know whose darling that is—don't you?
eyes so blue, And I know, etc.
pass from our view, And I know, etc.
wait - ing too, And I know, etc.
love so true, And I know, etc.

No. 109.   TITLE CLEAR.
R. S. CRANDALL.

1. Since I can read my ti-tle clear To mansions in the skies,
2. Should earth against my soul engage, And fi-ery darts be hurled,

I'll bid farewell to ev-ery fear, And wipe my weeping eyes.
Then I would smile at Satan's rage, And face a frowning world.

I'll bid farewell, etc.
Then I would smile, etc.

3 Let cares, like a wild deluge come,
  And storms of sorrow fall,
  May I but safely reach my home,
  My God, my heaven, my all.

4 There shall I bathe my weary soul
  In seas of heavenly rest,
  And not a wave of trouble roll
  Across my peaceful breast.

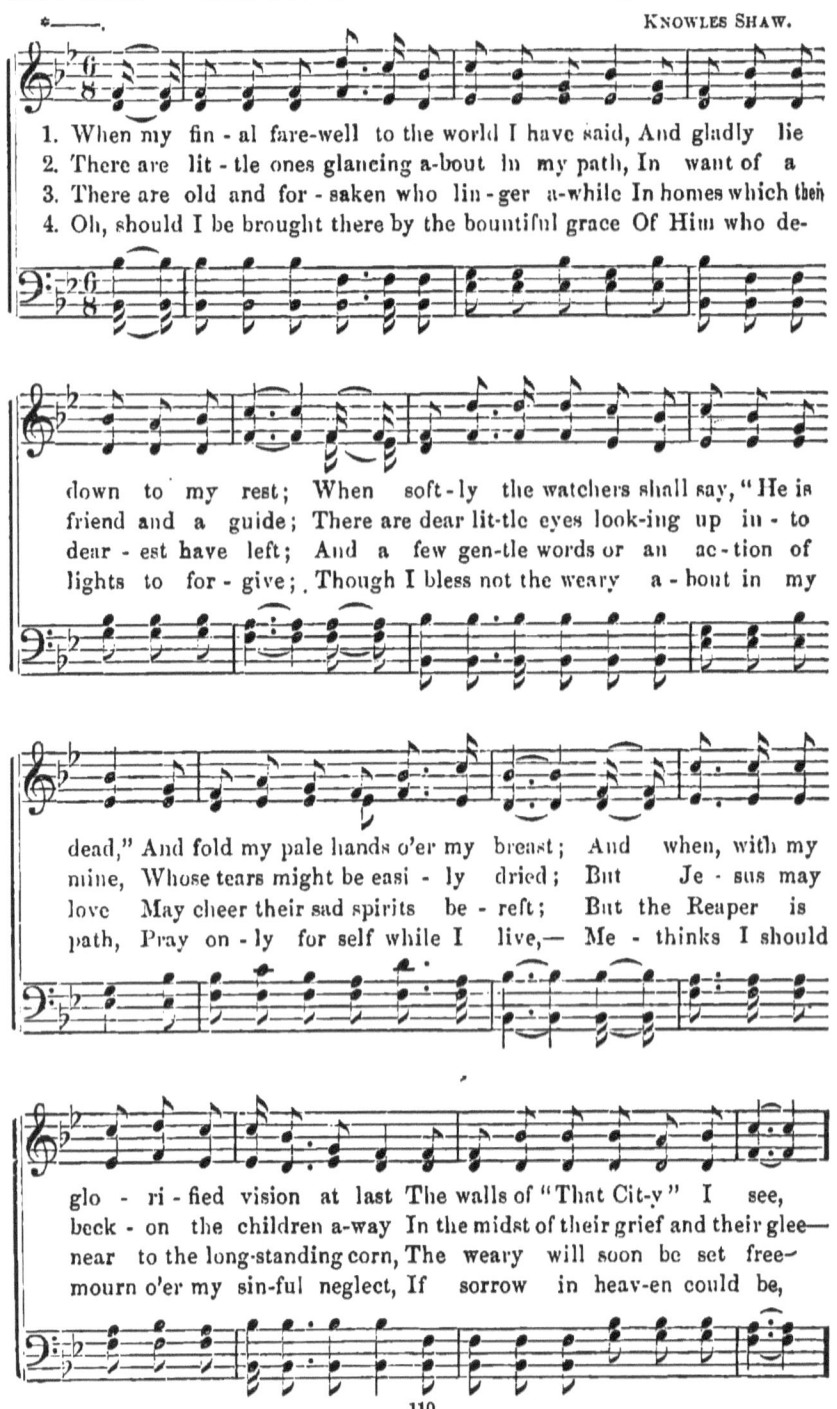

WAITING AND WATCHING. Concluded.

1–3. Will an-y one then at the beau-ti-ful gate, Be waiting and
4. Should no one I love at the beau-ti-ful gate, Be waiting and

CHORUS.

watching for me? Be waiting and watching for me? .... Be
watching for me; Be waiting and watching for me; .... Be

Be waiting and watching, be waiting for me? Be

wait-ing and watch-ing for me? .... Will an-y one
wait-ing and watch-ing for me; .... Should no one I

wait-ing and watch-ing, be watching for me?

Rit.

then at the beau-ti-ful gate, Be wait-ing and watching for me?
love at the beau-ti-ful gate, Be wait-ing and watching for me.

No. 111. SCATTER SEEDS OF KINDNESS.

"Whatsoever a man soweth, that shall he also reap."—Gal. 6: 7.

MRS. SMITH. S. J. VAIL.

1. Let us gather up the sunbeams, Lying all a-long our path; Let us
2. Strange, we never prize the music Till the sweet-voiced bird has flown! Strange, that
3. If we knew the baby fingers, Press'd against the window-pane, Would be
4. Ah! those little ice-cold fingers, How they point our mem'ries back To the

keep the wheat and roses, Cast-ing out the thorns and chaff; Let us
we should slight the violets Till the love-ly flowers are gone! Strange, that
cold and stiff to-morrow, Nev-er trouble us a - gain— Would the
has - ty word and actions, Strewn along our backward track! How those

find our sweetest comfort In the blessings of to - day; With a
summer skies and sunshine Nev-er seem one-half so fair, As when
bright eyes of our dar-ling Catch the frown upon our brow? Would the
lit - tle hands re-mind us, As in snowy grace they lie, Not to

By permission of PHILIP PHILLIPS.

SCATTER SEEDS OF KINDNESS. Concluded.

pa - tient hand re - moving All the bri - ars from the way.
win-ter's snow-y pinions Shake the white down in the air.
print of ro - sy fingers Vex us then as they do now?
scatter thorns, but roses— For our reap-ing by and by!

CHORUS.

Then scat-ter seeds of kind-ness, Then scat-ter seeds of kindness;

Then scat-ter seeds of kindness, For our reaping by and by.

No. 112. "WHITER THAN SNOW."

"Wash me thoroughly from mine iniquity."—Ps. 51: 2.

K. SHAW. KNOWLES SHAW.

DUET.

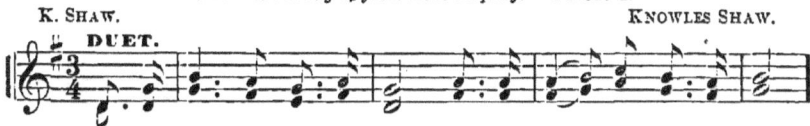

1. I am sin - ful, Lord, to Thee, In my an - guish I would flee;
2. Blind and lost I call for aid, Let Thy hand on me be laid;
3. Cleanse me in Thy precious blood, Love's pure crimson streaming flood;

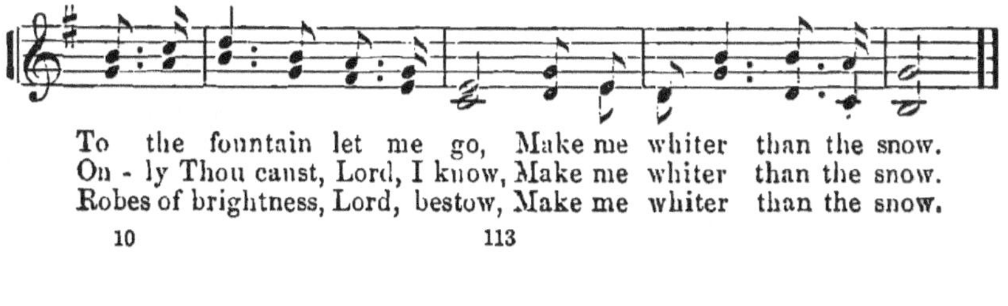

To the fountain let me go, Make me whiter than the snow.
On - ly Thou canst, Lord, I know, Make me whiter than the snow.
Robes of brightness, Lord, bestow, Make me whiter than the snow.

No. 114.   "PASS ME NOT"

Anon.   R. S. Crandall.

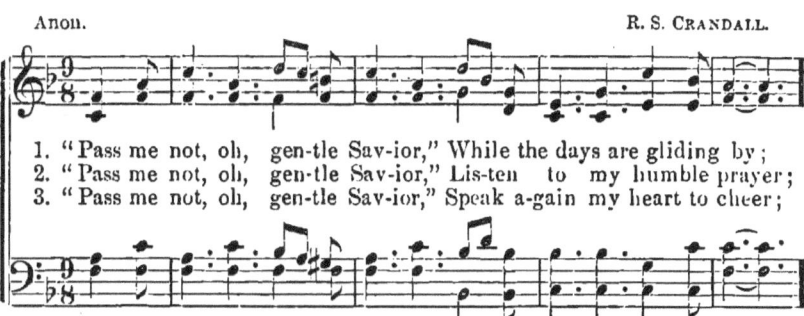

1. "Pass me not, oh, gen-tle Sav-ior," While the days are gliding by;
2. "Pass me not, oh, gen-tle Sav-ior," Lis-ten to my humble prayer;
3. "Pass me not, oh, gen-tle Sav-ior," Speak a-gain my heart to cheer;

D.C. "Pass me not, oh, gen-tle Sav-ior," Speak a-gain my heart to cheer;

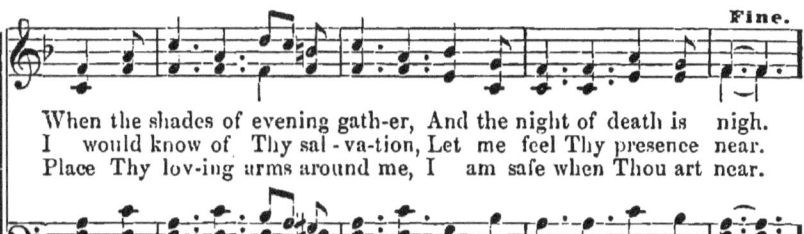

When the shades of evening gath-er, And the night of death is nigh.
I would know of Thy sal-va-tion, Let me feel Thy presence near.
Place Thy lov-ing arms around me, I am safe when Thou art near.

Place Thy lov-ing arms around me, I am safe when Thou art near.

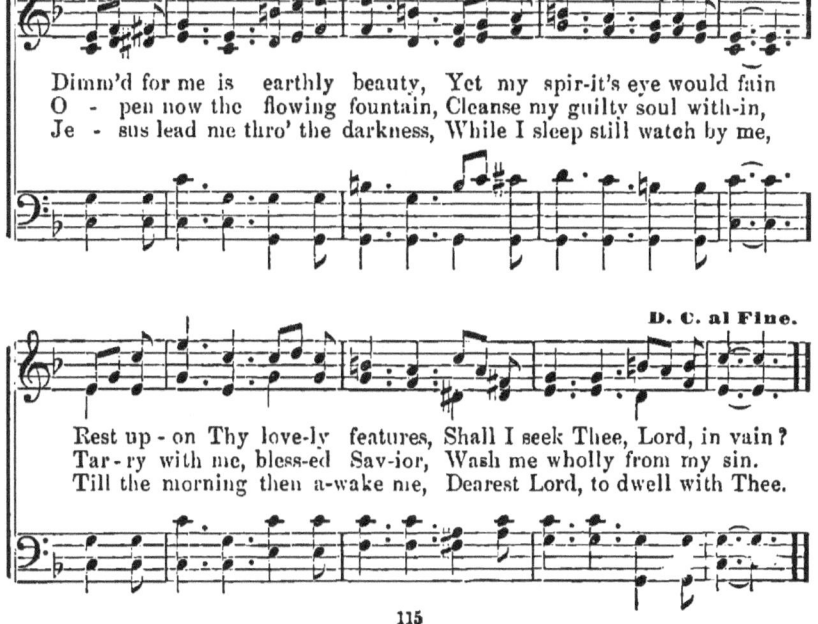

Dimm'd for me is earthly beauty, Yet my spir-it's eye would fain
O-pen now the flowing fountain, Cleanse my guilty soul with-in,
Je-sus lead me thro' the darkness, While I sleep still watch by me,

D. C. al Fine.

Rest up-on Thy love-ly features, Shall I seek Thee, Lord, in vain?
Tar-ry with me, bless-ed Sav-ior, Wash me wholly from my sin.
Till the morning then a-wake me, Dearest Lord, to dwell with Thee.

THE HANDWRITING ON THE WALL. Concluded.

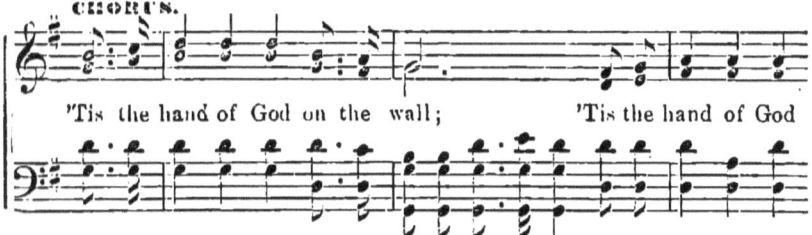

'Tis the hand of God on the wall; 'Tis the hand of God
'Tis the hand of God that is writing on the wall; 'Tis the hand of God

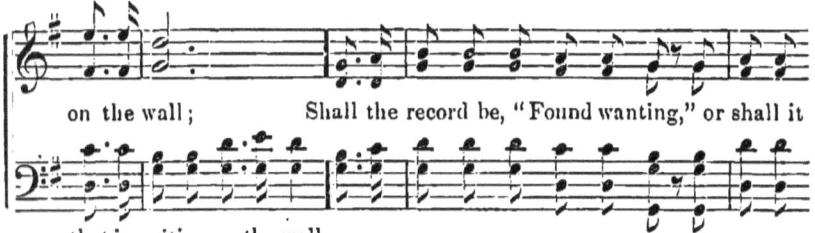

on the wall; Shall the record be, "Found wanting," or shall it
that is writing on the wall.

be, "Found trusting?" While that hand is writing on the wall,
writing on the wall.

No. 116.

1 Shout the tidings of salvation,
   To the aged and the young;
Till the precious invitation
   Waken every heart and tongue.
      CHORUS.
   Send the sound
     The earth around,
From the rising to the setting of the sun;
   Till each gathering crowd
     Shall proclaim aloud,
The glorious work is done!

2 Shout the tidings of salvation
   O'er the prairies of the west;
Till each gathering congregation,
   With the gospel sound is blest.

3 Shout the tidings of salvation,
   Mingling with the ocean's roar;
Till the ships of every nation,
   Bear the news from shore to shore.

No. 117.

1 Come, you sinners, poor and needy,
   Weak and wounded, sick and sore;
Jesus ready stands to save you,
   Full of pity, love, and power;
     He is able,
He is willing—doubt no more.

2 Let not conscience make you linger,
   Nor of fitness fondly dream;
All the fitness He requireth,
   Is to feel your need of Him;
     This He gives you,
'Tis the Savior's rising beam.

3 Come, you weary, heavy laden,
   Bruised and mangled by the fall;
If you tarry till you're better,
   You will never come at all;
     Not the righteous—
Sinners, Jesus came to call.

STANDING BY THE CROSS. Concluded.

No. 119.

1 Jesus, lover of my soul,
　Let me to Thy bosom fly,
While the billows near me roll,
　While the tempest still is high;
Hide me, oh, my Savior, hide,
　Till the storm of life is past,
Safe into the haven guide,
　Oh, receive my soul at last.

2 Other refuge have I none,
　Hangs my helpless soul on thee!
Leave, oh, leave me not alone,
　Still support and comfort me;
All my trust on Thee is stayed,
　All my help from Thee I bring,
Cover my defenseless head
　With the shadow of Thy wing.

3 Plenteous grace with Thee is found,
　Grace to pardon all my sins;
Let the healing streams abound,
　Make and keep me pure within.
Thou of life the fountain art,
　Freely let me take of Thee;
Spring Thou up within my heart,
　Rise to all eternity.

No. 120.

1 When we hear the music ringing
　In the bright, celestial dome,
When sweet angel voices singing,
　Gladly bid us welcome home
To the land of ancient story,
　Where the spirit knows no care,
In that land of light and glory,
　Shall we know each other there?

2 When the holy angels meet us,
　As we go to join their band,
Shall we know the friends that greet us
　In that glorious spirit land?
Shall we see the same eyes shining
　On us as in days of yore?
Shall we feel their dear arms twining
　Fondly round us as before?

3 Oh, ye weary, sad, and tossed ones,
　Droop not, faint not by the way;
You shall join the loved and just ones
　In the land of perfect day.
Harp-strings, touched by angel fingers,
　Murmured, in my raptured ear—
Evermore their sweet song lingers—
　We shall know each other there.

No. 97. "IF I WERE A VOICE."

KNOWLES SHAW.

SOLO. MELODY.

1. If I were a voice, a persuasive voice, That could travel this wide world
2. If I were a voice, a consoling voice, I would fly on the wings of the
3. If I were a voice, an immortal voice, That could travel this wide world

through; I would fly on the beams of the morning light, I would
air; The homes of sor-row and guilt I'd seek, And
round; Wher-ev-er man to his idols bowed, I'd

speak to men with a gentle might, I'd tell them to be true.
calm and truth-ful words I'd speak, To save them from des-pair.
publish in notes both long and loud, The gos-pel's joy-ful sound.

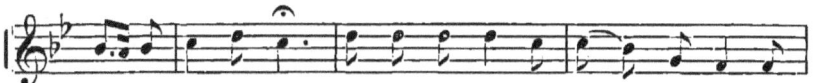

I would fly, I would fly o-ver land and sea, Wher-ev-er a
I would fly, I would fly o'er the crowded town, I'd drop like the
I would fly, I would fly on the wings of day, Proclaiming peace

hu-man heart could be; Tell-ing a tale, or sing-ing a song, In
hap-py sunbeam down In-to the hearts of suf-fer-ing men, I'd
on my world-wide way; Bidding this saddened earth re-joice, If

CHORUS.

praise of the right, or in blame of the wrong.
teach them to look up a-gain. I would fly, .. I would
I were a voice, an im-mor-tal voice.

fly, I would fly, .. I would fly, I would fly over land and sea.

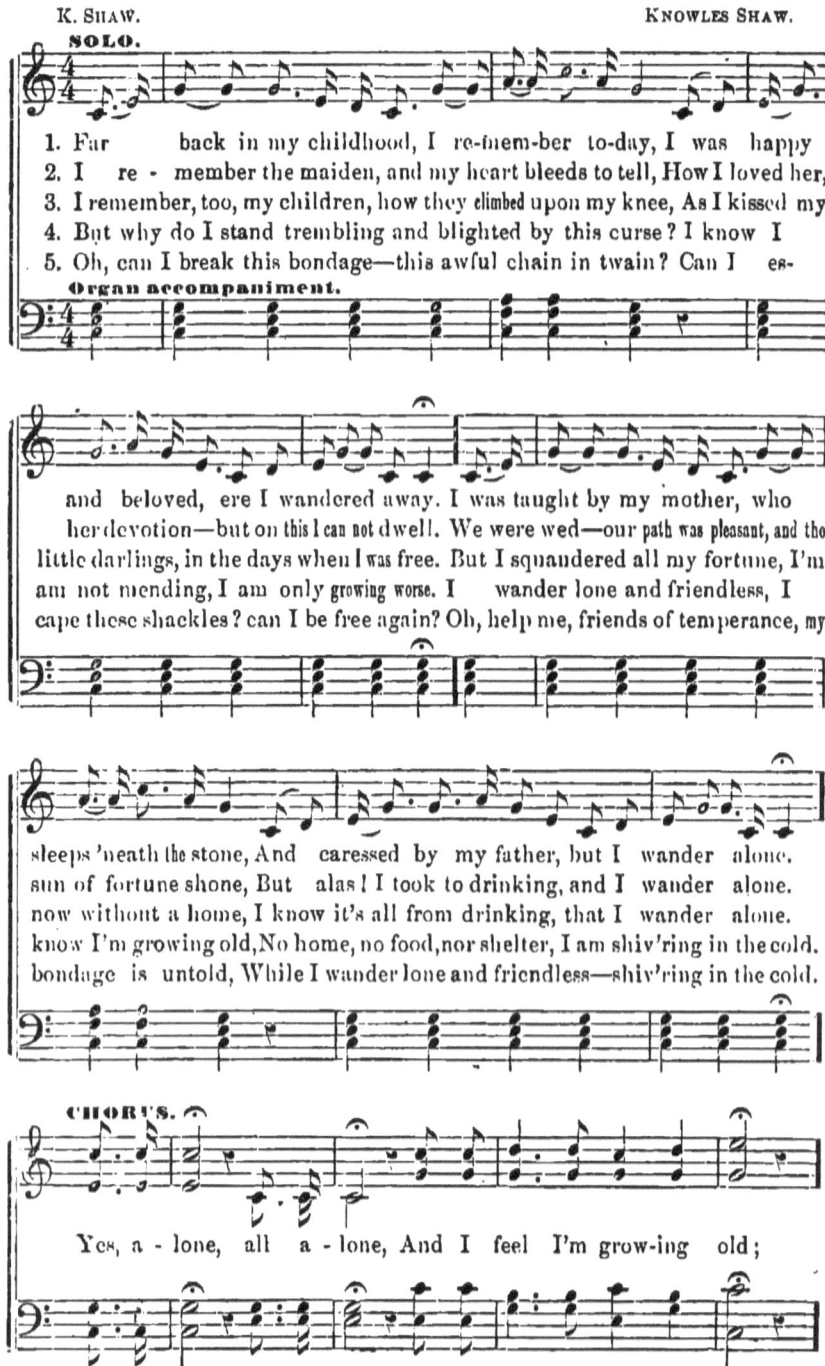

SHIVERING IN THE COLD. Concluded.

Yet I wan-der, oh, how lone-ly, I am shiv'ring in the cold.

No. 99. CHRIST, THE ONLY WAY.

"I am the way, the truth, and the life."—John 14: 6.

K. SHAW.   KNOWLES SHAW.

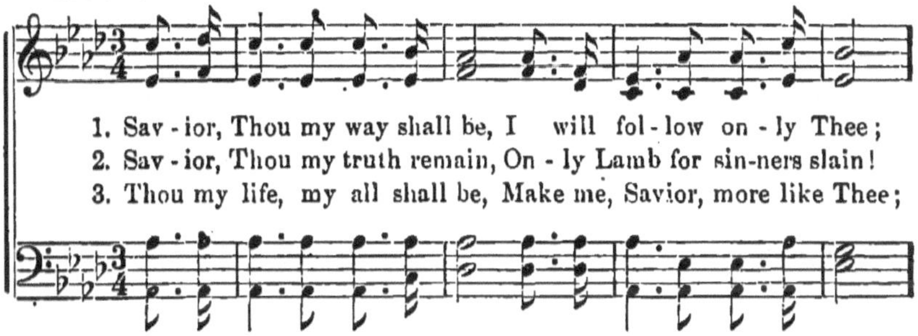

1. Sav-ior, Thou my way shall be, I will fol-low on-ly Thee;
2. Sav-ior, Thou my truth remain, On-ly Lamb for sin-ners slain!
3. Thou my life, my all shall be, Make me, Savior, more like Thee;

Be Thou near me night and day, Sav-ior, Thou, the on-ly way.
Take a-way my guilt, I pray, Sav-ior, Thou, the on-ly way.
Give me joy in end-less day, Sav-ior, Thou, the on-ly way.

CHORUS.   Rep. *pp*

Lead me on by night and day, Savior, Thou, the on-ly way.

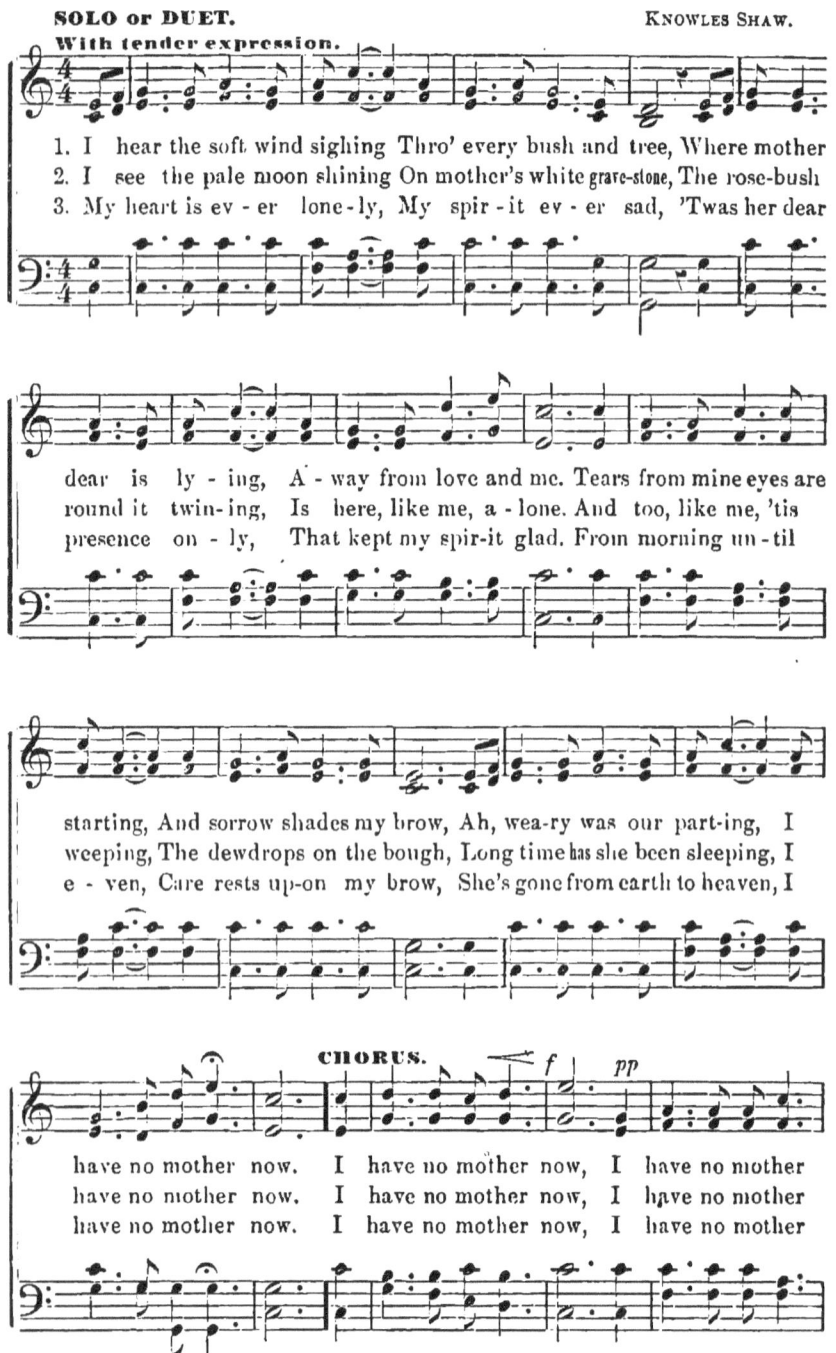

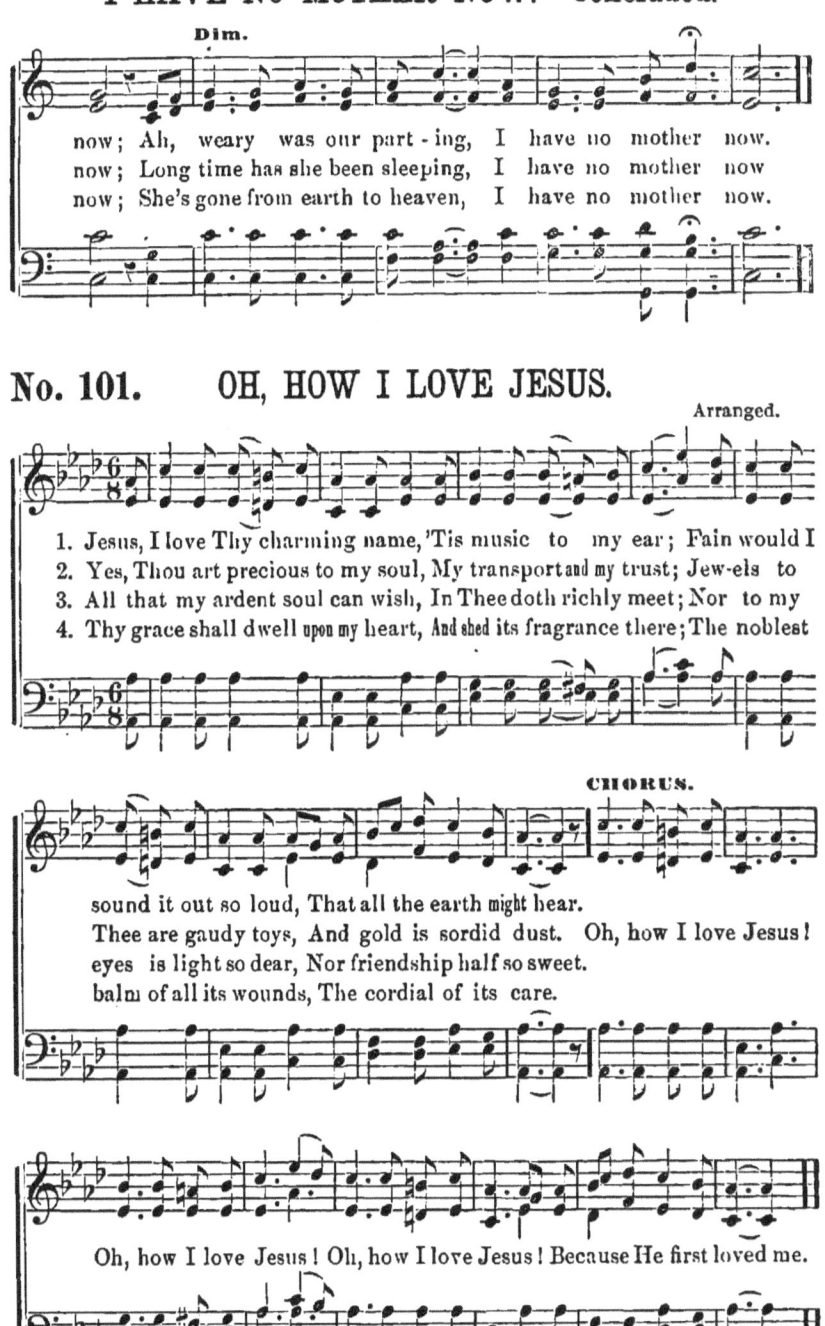

No. 104. SONG OF WELCOME.

K. S. (CONCERT OPENING PIECE.) KNOWLES SHAW.

104

SONG OF WELCOME. Concluded.

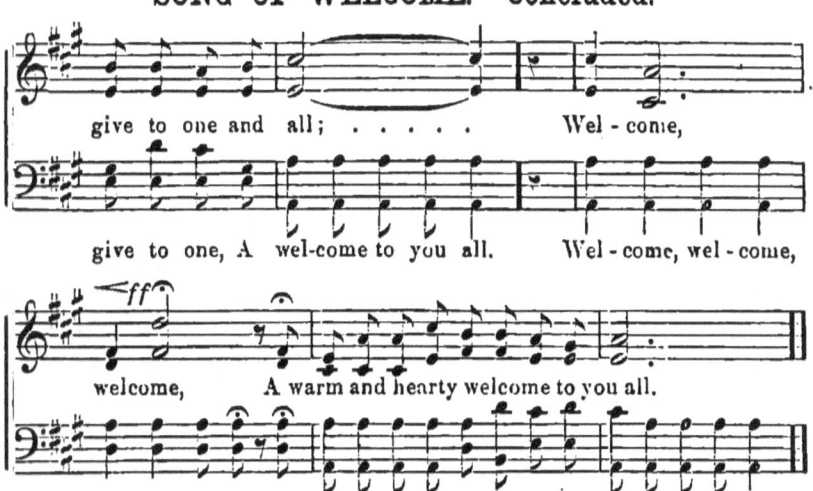

No. 105.   "MY AIN COUNTRIE."
Scotch Melody.

SOLO.

1. { I am far frae my hame, an' I'm weary aftenwhiles, For my
    { An' I'll ne'er be fu' con-tent, un - til my een do see The
D. C. But these sichts an' these soun's will as naething be to me, When I

lang'd-for hame-bringing, an' my Father's welcome smiles,
gowden gates of heaven, an' my . . . . . ain countrie.
hear the angels sing-ing in my . . . . . ain countrie.

{ The earth is fleck'd with flowers, mony - tinted, fresh and gay; }
{ The bird-ies sing-ing blithely, for my Father made them sae; }

  2 I've his gude word of promise that some gladsome day, the King
    To His ain royal palace, His banished hame will bring.
    Wi' een an' wi' heart flowing owre, we shall see
    "The King in His beauty," in His ain countrie.
    My sins hae been mony, an' my sorrows hae been sair:
    But there they'll never vex me, nor be remembered mair:
    His bluid hath made me white, an' His hand shall wipe my ee',
    When He brings me hame at last to my ain countrie.

  3 Like a bairn to its mither, a wee birdie to its nest,
    I fain wad noo be ganging unto my Savior's breast,
    For He gathers in His bosom, witless, worthless lambs like me,
    He "carries them Himsel'," to His ain countrie.
    He's faithfu' that has promised, He'll surely come again,
    He'll keep His tryst wi' me, at what hour I dinna ken;
    But He bids me still to wait, an' ready aye to be,
    To gang at ony moment, to His ain countrie.

"DRIFTING AWAY." Concluded.

know you are drift - ing a - way; But oh, as I see you
night, while you're drifting a - way; A - lone with the night, for
know you are drift - ing a - way; But oh, as I see you
ters that spar - kle a - bove; But drift with its soul once

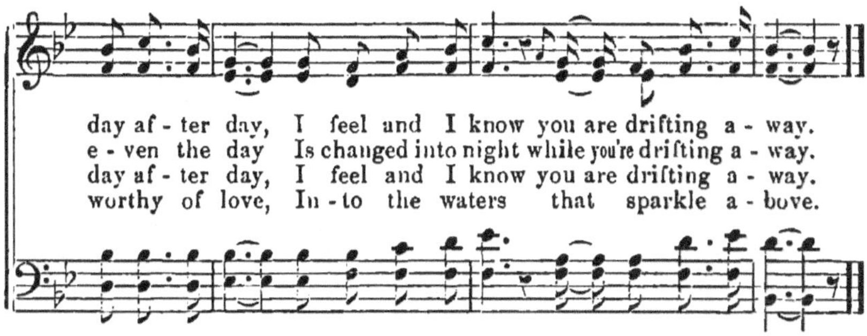

day af - ter day, I feel and I know you are drifting a - way.
e - ven the day Is changed into night while you're drifting a - way.
day af - ter day, I feel and I know you are drifting a - way.
worthy of love, In - to the waters that sparkle a - bove.

No. 107. BROAD IS THE ROAD.

DANIEL READ.

1. Broad is the road that leads to death, And thousands walk together there,
2. "Deny thyself, and take thy cross," Is the Redeemer's great command;
3. The fearful soul that tires and faints, And walks the ways of God no more,
4. Lord, let not all my hopes be vain, Cre - ate my heart en - tirely new—

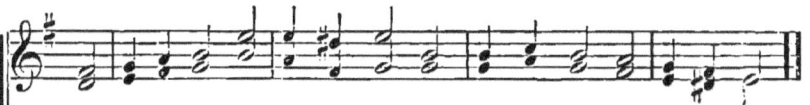

But wisdom shows a narrow path, With here and there a trav-el-er.
Nature must count her gold but dross, If she would gain this heavenly land.
Is but esteemed almost a saint, And makes his own destruction sure.
Which hypocrites could ne'er attain, Which false a-pos-tates never knew.

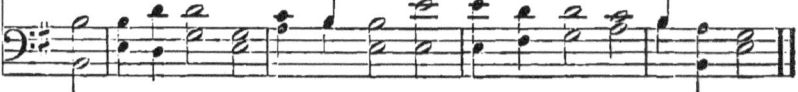

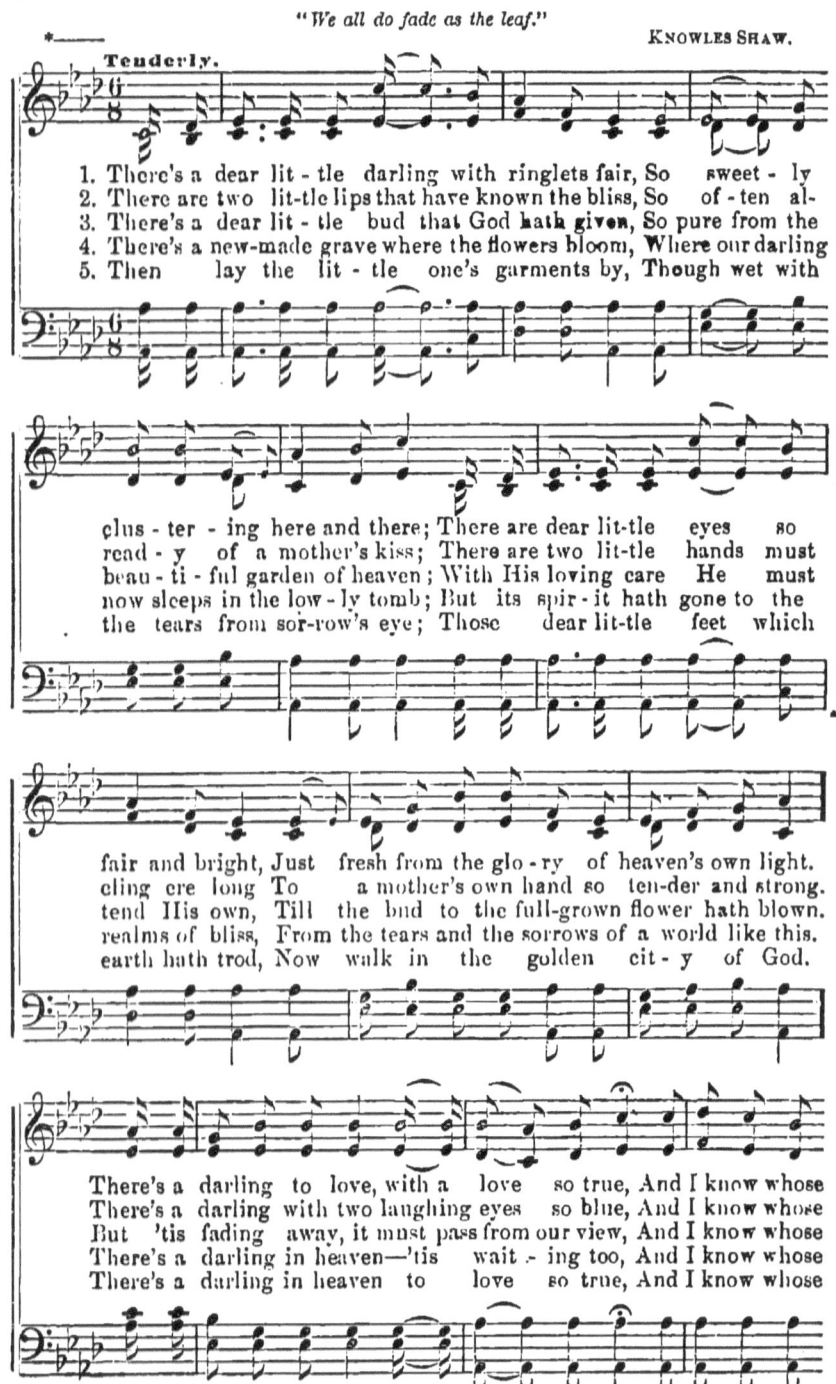

OUR DEAR LITTLE DARLING. Concluded.

darling that is—don't you? There's a dar-ling to love with a
darling that is—don't you? There's a dar-ling with two laughing
darling that is—don't you? But 'tis fad-ing a-way, it must
darling that is—don't you? There's a dar-ling in heaven—'tis
darling that is—don't you? There's a dar-ling in heaven to

love so true, And I know whose darling that is—don't you?
eyes so blue, And I know, etc.
pass from our view, And I know, etc.
wait - ing too, And I know, etc.
love so true, And I know, etc.

No. 109.   TITLE CLEAR.   R. S. CRANDALL.

1. Since I can read my ti-tle clear To mansions in the skies,
2. Should earth against my soul engage, And fi-ery darts be hurled,

I'll bid farewell to ev-ery fear, And wipe my weeping eyes.
Then I would smile at Satan's rage, And face a frowning world.

I'll bid farewell, etc.
Then I would smile, etc.

3 Let cares, like a wild deluge come,
 And storms of sorrow fall,
 May I but safely reach my home,
 My God, my heaven, my all.

4 There shall I bathe my weary soul
 In seas of heavenly rest,
 And not a wave of trouble roll
 Across my peaceful breast.

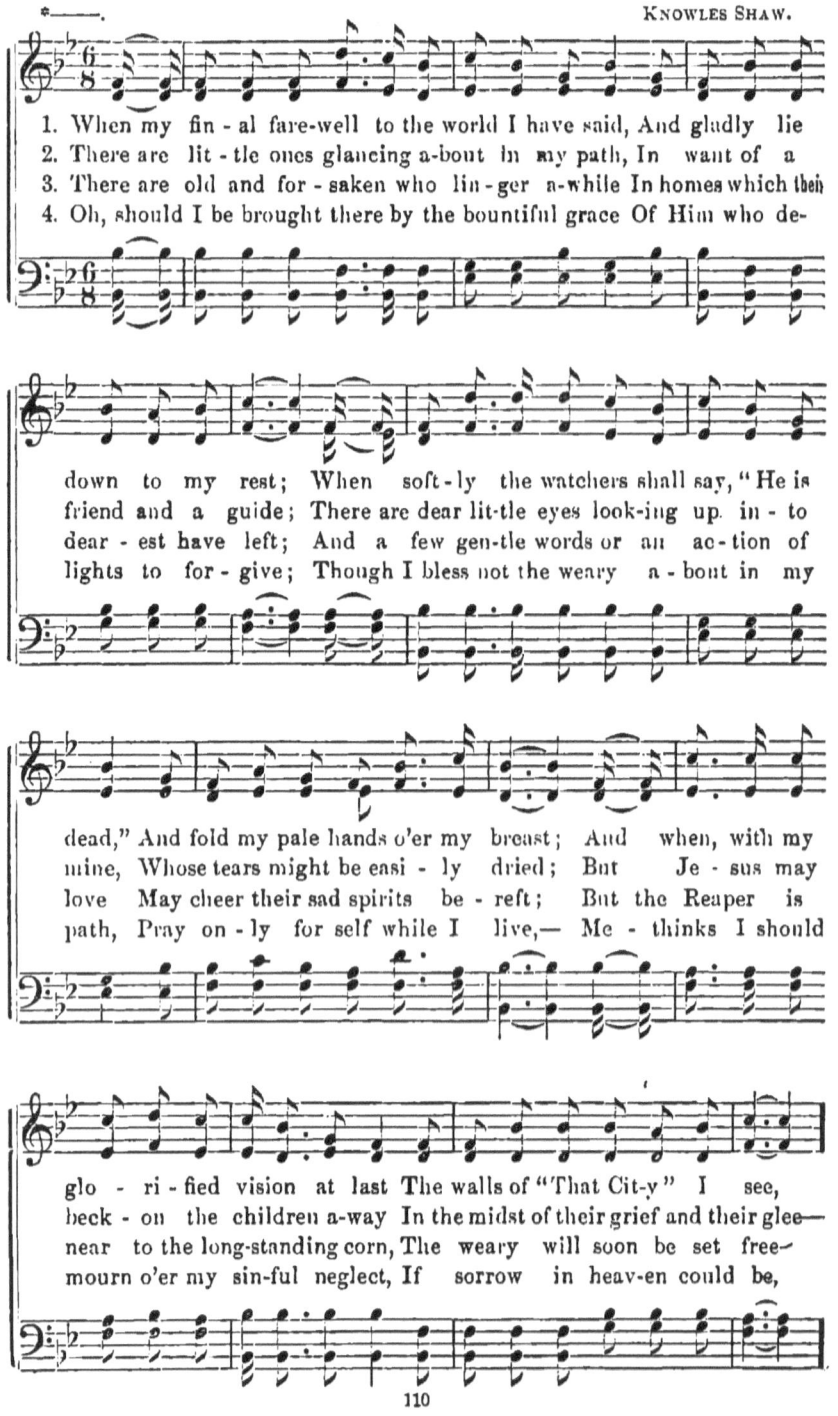

WAITING AND WATCHING. Concluded.

No. 111. SCATTER SEEDS OF KINDNESS.

"Whatsoever a man soweth, that shall he also reap."—Gal. 6: 7.

MRS. SMITH.   S. J. VAIL.

1. Let us gather up the sunbeams, Lying all a-long our path; Let us
2. Strange, we never prize the music Till the sweet-voiced bird has flown! Strange, that
3. If we knew the baby fingers, Press'd against the window-pane, Would be
4. Ah! those little ice-cold fingers, How they point our mem'ries back To the

keep the wheat and roses, Cast-ing out the thorns and chaff; Let us
we should slight the violets Till the love-ly flowers are gone! Strange, that
cold and stiff to-morrow, Nev-er trouble us a-gain— Would the
has-ty word and actions, Strewn along our backward track! How those

find our sweetest comfort In the blessings of to-day; With a
summer skies and sunshine Nev-er seem one-half so fair, As when
bright eyes of our dar-ling Catch the frown upon our brow? Would the
lit-tle hands re-mind us, As in snowy grace they lie, Not to

By permission of PHILIP PHILLIPS.

SCATTER SEEDS OF KINDNESS. Concluded.

pa-tient hand re-moving All the bri-ars from the way.
win-ter's snow-y pinions Shake the white down in the air.
print of ro-sy fingers Vex us then as they do now?
scatter thorns, but roses— For our reap-ing by and by!

CHORUS.

Then scat-ter seeds of kind-ness, Then scat-ter seeds of kindness;

Then scat-ter seeds of kindness, For our reaping by and by.

No. 112. "WHITER THAN SNOW."

"Wash me thoroughly from mine iniquity."—Ps. 51: 2.

K. SHAW.   KNOWLES SHAW.

DUET.

1. I am sin-ful, Lord, to Thee, In my an-guish I would flee;
2. Blind and lost I call for aid, Let Thy hand on me be laid;
3. Cleanse me in Thy precious blood, Love's pure crimson streaming flood;

To the fountain let me go, Make me whiter than the snow.
On-ly Thou canst, Lord, I know, Make me whiter than the snow.
Robes of brightness, Lord, bestow, Make me whiter than the snow.

No. 114. "PASS ME NOT"

Anon.
R. S. Crandall.

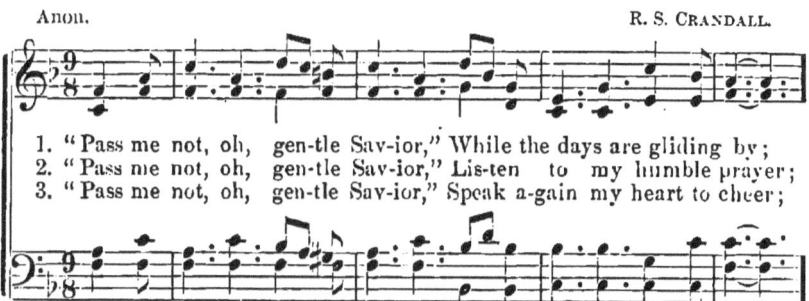

1. "Pass me not, oh, gen-tle Sav-ior," While the days are gliding by;
2. "Pass me not, oh, gen-tle Sav-ior," Lis-ten to my humble prayer;
3. "Pass me not, oh, gen-tle Sav-ior," Speak a-gain my heart to cheer;

D.C. "Pass me not, oh, gen-tle Sav-ior," Speak a-gain my heart to cheer;

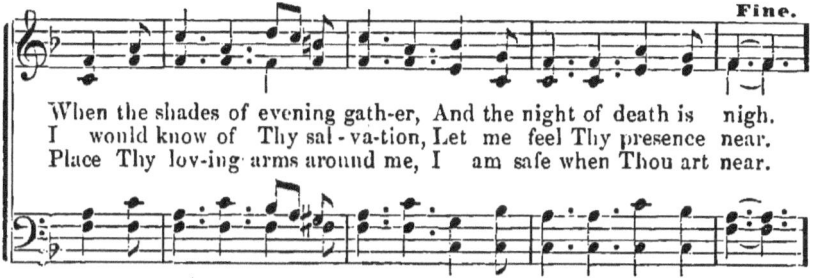

Fine.

When the shades of evening gath-er, And the night of death is nigh.
I would know of Thy sal-va-tion, Let me feel Thy presence near.
Place Thy lov-ing arms around me, I am safe when Thou art near.

Place Thy lov-ing arms around me, I am safe when Thou art near.

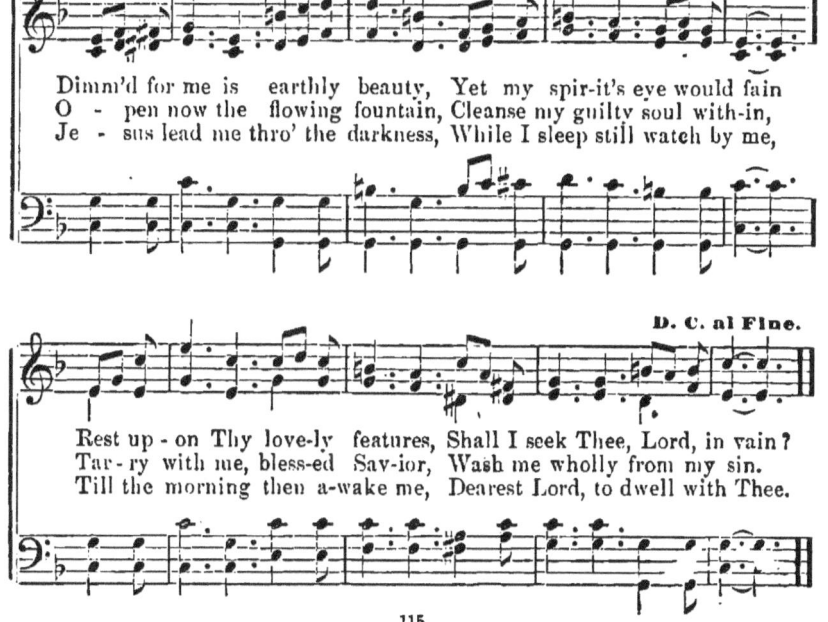

Dimm'd for me is earthly beauty, Yet my spir-it's eye would fain
O - pen now the flowing fountain, Cleanse my guilty soul with-in,
Je - sus lead me thro' the darkness, While I sleep still watch by me,

D. C. al Fine.

Rest up-on Thy love-ly features, Shall I seek Thee, Lord, in vain?
Tar-ry with me, bless-ed Sav-ior, Wash me wholly from my sin.
Till the morning then a-wake me, Dearest Lord, to dwell with Thee.

No. 115. THE HANDWRITING ON THE WALL.

"And the king saw the part of the hand that wrote."—Dan. 5: 5.

K. Shaw.   Knowles Shaw.

1. At the feast of Bel-shaz-zar and a thousand of his lords,
2. See the brave cap-tive Dan-iel as he stood be-fore the throng,
3. See the faith, zeal, and cour-age, that would dare to do the right,
4. So our deeds are re-cord-ed—there's a Hand that's writing now,

While they drank from golden vessels, as the book of truth re-cords;
And rebuked the haughty monarch for his might-y deeds of wrong;
Which the spir-it gave to Daniel—this the se-cret of his might;
Sin-ner, give your heart to Je-sus, to His roy-al man-date bow;

In the night as they rev-el in the roy-al pal-ace hall,
As he read out the writing—'twas the doom of one and all,
In his home in Ju-de-a, or a cap-tive in the hall—
For the day is ap-proaching— it must come to one and all,

They were seized with consternation, 'twas the hand up-on the wall.
For the kingdom now was finished—said the hand up-on the wall.
He un-der-stood the writing of his God up-on the wall.
When the sinner's con-dem-na-tion, will be writ-ten on the wall.

THE HANDWRITING ON THE WALL. Concluded.

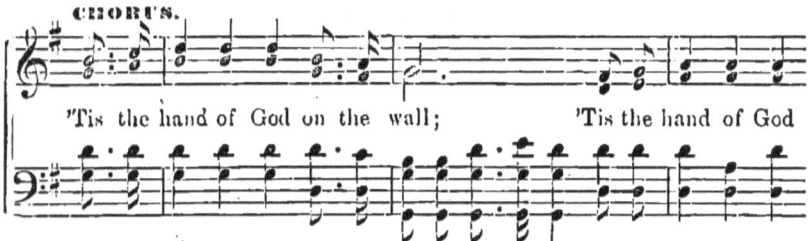

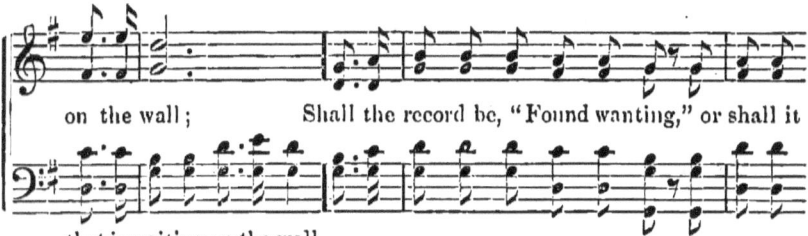

No. 116.

1 Shout the tidings of salvation,
  To the aged and the young;
  Till the precious invitation
  Waken every heart and tongue.

CHORUS.

  Send the sound
  The earth around,
From the rising to the setting of the sun;
  Till each gathering crowd
  Shall proclaim aloud,
The glorious work is done!

2 Shout the tidings of salvation
  O'er the prairies of the west;
  Till each gathering congregation,
  With the gospel sound is blest.

3 Shout the tidings of salvation,
  Mingling with the ocean's roar;
  Till the ships of every nation,
  Bear the news from shore to shore.

No. 117.

1 Come, you sinners, poor and needy,
  Weak and wounded, sick and sore;
  Jesus ready stands to save you,
  Full of pity, love, and power;
    He is able,
  He is willing—doubt no more.

2 Let not conscience make you linger,
  Nor of fitness fondly dream;
  All the fitness He requireth,
  Is to feel your need of Him;
    This He gives you,
  'Tis the Savior's rising beam.

3 Come, you weary, heavy laden,
  Bruised and mangled by the fall;
  If you tarry till you're better,
  You will never come at all;
    Not the righteous—
  Sinners, Jesus came to call.

STANDING BY THE CROSS. Concluded.

all ye lov-ers of the Lord; Be read-y for the strife, at the bidding of His word; Let the world with all its charms be counted on-ly dross; Ready then to do or die, standing by the cross.

No. 119.

1 Jesus, lover of my soul,
  Let me to Thy bosom fly,
While the billows near me roll,
  While the tempest still is high;
Hide me, oh, my Savior, hide,
  Till the storm of life is past,
Safe into the haven guide,
  Oh, receive my soul at last.

2 Other refuge have I none,
  Hangs my helpless soul on thee!
Leave, oh, leave me not alone,
  Still support and comfort me;
All my trust on Thee is stayed,
  All my help from Thee I bring,
Cover my defenseless head
  With the shadow of Thy wing.

3 Plenteous grace with Thee is found,
  Grace to pardon all my sins;
Let the healing streams abound,
  Make and keep me pure within.
Thou of life the fountain art,
  Freely let me take of Thee;
Spring Thou up within my heart,
  Rise to all eternity.

No. 120.

1 When we hear the music ringing
  In the bright, celestial dome,
When sweet angel voices singing,
  Gladly bid us welcome home
To the land of ancient story,
  Where the spirit knows no care,
In that land of light and glory,
  Shall we know each other there?

2 When the holy angels meet us,
  As we go to join their band,
Shall we know the friends that greet us
  In that glorious spirit land?
Shall we see the same eyes shining
  On us as in days of yore?
Shall we feel their dear arms twining
  Fondly round us as before?

3 Oh, ye weary, sad, and tossed ones,
  Droop not, faint not by the way;
You shall join the loved and just ones
  In the land of perfect day.
Harp-strings, touched by angel fingers,
  Murmured, in my raptured ear—
Evermore their sweet song lingers—
  We shall know each other there.

THE GREAT WHITE THRONE. Concluded.

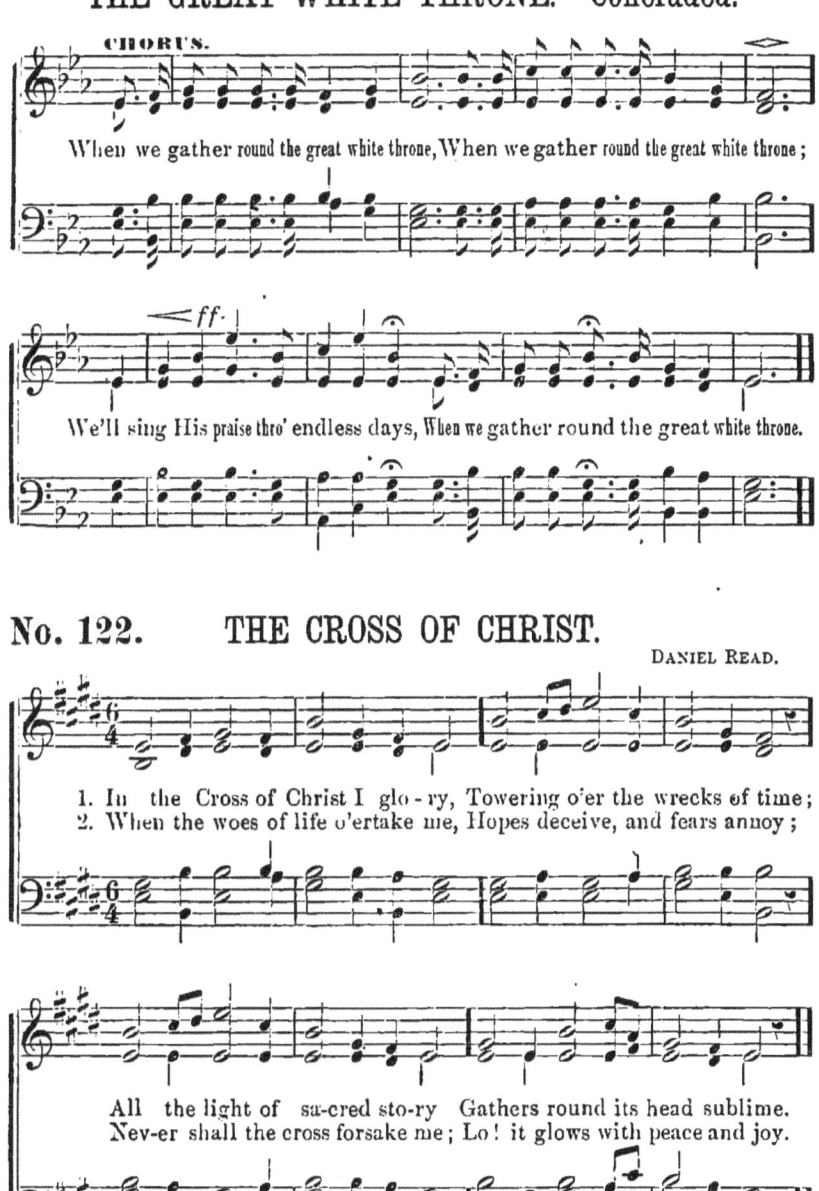

When we gather round the great white throne, When we gather round the great white throne;
We'll sing His praise thro' endless days, When we gather round the great white throne.

No. 122.   THE CROSS OF CHRIST.
DANIEL READ.

1. In the Cross of Christ I glory, Towering o'er the wrecks of time;
2. When the woes of life o'ertake me, Hopes deceive, and fears annoy;

All the light of sacred story Gathers round its head sublime.
Nev-er shall the cross forsake me; Lo! it glows with peace and joy.

3 When the sun of bliss is beaming
 Light and love upon my way,
 From the cross the radiance streaming
 Adds new luster to the day.

4 Bane and blessing, pain and pleasure,
 By the cross are sanctified;
 Peace is there, that knows no measure,
 Joys that through all time abide.

THE KING IN HIS BEAUTY. Concluded.

No. 124. THE THREE CALLS.

The "Third," "Sixth and Ninth," and "Eleventh Hour."—Matt. 20: 3, 5, 6.

I. B. WOODBURY.

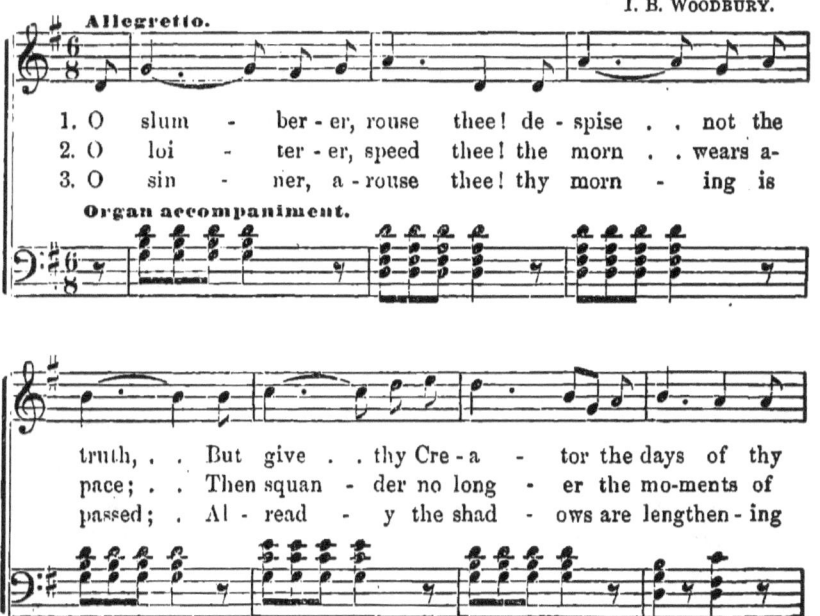

1. O slum - ber - er, rouse thee! de - spise . . not the truth, . . But give . . thy Cre - a - tor the days of thy
2. O loi - ter - er, speed thee! the morn . . wears a-pace; . . Then squan - der no long - er the mo-ments of
3. O sin - ner, a - rouse thee! thy morn - ing is passed; . . Al - read - y the shad - ows are lengthen - ing

By permission of O. DITSON & Co.

THE THREE CALLS. Concluded.

No. 125. "I'S LOOTIN' OUT FOR YOU."

Arranged. KNOWLES SHAW.

With expression.

1. My lit-tle dar-ling used to stand Just by my cot-tage
2. She was my joy, my heart's de-light, In those days long gone
3. A-las! how lone-ly now our life, As through the world we
4. Yet oh, what com-fort to my heart, That when I'm called a-

door; Waiting to kiss me when I came Each evening from the
by; But as I'm dreaming o'er the past, A tear comes in my
roam, Since no sweet voice calls out to me, To bid me wel-come
way From toils be-low to joys a-bove, In heaven's e-ter-nal

store; Her eyes were like two love-ly stars, That shine in heav'n's own
eye; She calls no more when I come home, As oft she used to
home. No loving arms thrown round me now, No eyes so sweet-ly
day; That there she'll meet me at the gate, Just as I'm pass-ing

blue; "Papa," she'd call, "you see I's here, I's lootin' out for you."
do; "Papa," you see your darling's here, I's lootin' out for you."
blue, No voice now calls from cottage door, "I's lootin' out for you."
thro', "Papa," she'll call, with her sweet voice, "I's lootin' out for you."

CHORUS. *ff*   *pp*

"I's lootin' out for you, I's lootin' out for you, Pa-pa, you

see (Pa-pa,) your dar-ling's here, I's lootin' out for you."

By permission of JOHN CHURCH & Co., owners of copyright.

INDEX.

Title	NO.
At the tomb	9
All for thee	15
Any may come	32
A kingdom in glory	49
A home with Jesus	50
Always pray	94
Broad is the road	107
Blood bought	3
Bringing in the sheaves	82
Better further on	74
Beyond the dark sea	66
By and by	64
Bright, beautiful heaven	53
Beautiful dream	52
Born again	31
Be in our midst to-day	16
Come you sinners	117
Christ the only way	99
Come to-day	73
Cross and crown	37
Coronation	10
Come to Jesus	30
Come to the fount	27
Drifting away	106
Doubt no more	13
Doxology (Old Hundred)	79
From every stormy wind	93
Go to thy rest	103
Go thy way for this time	46
Go work in my vineyard	91
Happy day	85
Heavenly mansions	71
Happy pilgrims	55
Have mercy on me	44
Hosanna	113
I's lootin' out for you	125
I have no mother now	100
If I were a voice	97
If we knew	88
I love Jesus	76
Is it far?	62
I need thee, precious Jesus	34
If, Lord, thou callest me	22
Is it I?	19
I am the Vine	4
I love thy kingdom, Lord	47
Joy to the world!	33
Jesus, lover of my soul	119
Jesus on the sea	92
Just beyond	48
Jesus our Friend	11
Known to thee	45
Love for all	41
My ain countrie	105
Messenger angels	72
My soul, be on thy guard	35
My gracious Redeemer	18
My faith looks up to thee	7
Not much further to go	68
Nearer to thee	65
Not ashamed of Christ	43
Not far from the kingdom	40
Oh, how I love Jesus	101
Oh, for a closer walk	95
Overcome evil with good	83
Over the river	78
Out of the darkness	75
Only a little while	67
Oh, thou fount	51
One sweetly solemn thought	126
Our dear little darling	108
On the cross	6
Pass me not	114
Remember me	77
Redeemed	96
Rock of Ages	8
Shout the tidings	116
Scatter seeds of kindness	111
Song of welcome	104
Sweeping through the gates	102
Shivering in the cold	98
Standing by the cross	118
Sound the truth abroad	69
Shelter of safety	59
Salvation for all	38
Standing, knocking, waiting	26
Singing for Jesus	17
The King in his beauty	123
The three calls	124
The great white throne	121
The cross of Christ	122
The handwriting on the wall	115
Title clear	109
The barren fig tree	86
That beautiful land	70
The Savior is coming	63
The golden city	61
The happy beyond	58
The gospel banner	57
The other land	54
The land of promise	39
Tarry with me	25
The Savior's call	24
There is a fountain	23
To-day the Savior calls	20
The half has never been told	14
The manger of Bethlehem	5
The bright Morning Star	1
Valley of blessing	60
Will you go?	21
Whiter than snow	112
Waiting and watching	110
What will the harvest be	90
Work, for the night is coming	89
We praise thee, O God	87
When our ways	84
Watch	81
Waiting at the door	80
When the Comforter comes	56
Who shall be able to stand?	42
What say the bells	36
When shall we meet again?	29
Wandering away	28
We believe	12
What could we do without Jesus	2
When we hear the music ringing	120

www.ingramcontent.com/pod-product-compliance
Lightning Source LLC
Chambersburg PA
CBHW020112170426
43199CB00009B/503